Sunsu
(Bemba: to comfort, to cradle)

The story of the
Sisters of the
Sacred Hearts of Jesus and Mary in Zambia
1956 – 2006

Sisters of the Sacred Hearts of Jesus and Mary

*Let us praise illustrious people,
our ancestors in their successive generations...
whose good works have not been forgotten,
and whose names live on for all generations.*

Book of Ecclesiasticus, 44:1, 1

First published in the United Kingdom in 2014
by Sisters of the Sacred Hearts of Jesus and Mary

Text © 2014 Sisters of the Sacred Hearts of Jesus and Mary

ISBN 978-0-99295480-2

Production, cover design and page layout by Nick Snode (npsnode@btinternet.com)
Cover image by Michael Smith (dreamstime.com)
Typeset in Palatino 12.5/14.5pt
Printed and bound by www.printondemand-worldwide.com, Peterborough, UK

Contents

Foreword 5
To the reader 6
Mother Antonia 7
Chapter 1   Blazing the Trail 9
Chapter 2   Preparing the Way 19
Chapter 3   Making History 24
Chapter 4   Into Africa 32
Chapter 5   'Ladies in White' – Getting Started ... 42
Chapter 6   Historic Events 47
Chapter 7   'A Greater Sacrifice' 52
Bishop Adolph Furstenberg 55
Chapter 8   The Winds of Change 62
Map of Zambia 68
Chapter 9   Eventful Years 69
Chapter 10 On the Edge of a New Era 79

Chapter 11	'Energy and resourcefulness'	88
Chapter 12	Exploring New Ways	96
Chapter 13	Reading the Signs of the Times	108
Chapter 14	Handing Over	119
Chapter 15	Racing towards the Finish	126
Chapter 16	Into the Twenty First Century	146
Chapter 17	A Bold and Joyful Step Forward	158

Foreword

IT IS MY PRIVILEGE to introduce '*Sunsuntila*'. It is an excellent record of the history of our Mission in Zambia, from 1956 to 2006, and reflects fifty years of loving service carried out by our Sisters and all those who supported them in their mission.

The materials used in this history have obviously been well researched as it gives so much interesting detail on how the mission developed over the years. Certainly a lot of hard work has gone into its compilation.

I know you will find the story both interesting and enriching. The writing style makes it very readable indeed. As a Congregation we should be proud of what our Sisters have achieved in our Mission in Zambia, and how we helped to make Christ present to some of the poorest and most needy people.

On behalf of the Congregation, I would like to thank Sister Austin Gallagher for her enthusiasm and for the painstaking research she has put into such a beautiful book. She has spent many hours ensuring that all details are accurate.

Yours in Christ,
Sister Elizabeth Dawson
Congregational Leader
27th February 2014

To the reader

THIS BRIEF HISTORY of the Sisters of the Sacred Hearts of Jesus and Mary in Zambia, 1956-2006, could not have been written without the help of the Sisters who served in the past or who are still engaged in ministry there. Their names can be found in the footnotes at the end of each chapter. My thanks to all of them. To the priests and co-workers who generously sent me relevant information, I express my sincere gratitude. Special thanks to Sister Margaret Shanahan who willingly provided me with necessary materials from the Archives at Chigwell, and to my friend and former colleague. Dr. Enda Cully, who read and checked the text. My own time in Zambia during the 1960s has helped me to regard the writing of this story as an honour, and for this I am grateful to Sister Elizabeth Dawson, Congregational Leader.

Sister Brigid Gallagher

Feast of St. Margaret Mary,
16th October, 2013

REV. MOTHER ANTONIA PHILLIPS
1899 – 1974

Superior General of the Congregation of the
Sacred Hearts of Jesus and Mary, 1941-1963

Chapter 1

Blazing the Trail

> In our childhood days, Africa seemed a far-off continent and one we decided in our thoughts, we were never destined to see. Times have changed and now one can reach Central Africa in two days without any hardship – if one is brave enough to like air travel.[1]

WITH THESE WORDS Mother Antonia introduced her description of her first visit to Africa, from 6 to 25 September, 1954, in a circular letter to the Sisters of the Congregation of the Sacred Hearts of Jesus and Mary.[2] As its Superior General she was, in her own words, 'blazing the trail' in Central Africa to set up a new mission in what was then known as Northern Rhodesia (Zambia).

Mother Antonia had been invited by Bishop Joseph Van den Biesen,[3] Missionary of Africa, Vicar Apostolic of the Vicariate of Abercorn (now Mbala), to send Nursing Sisters, including midwives. to staff the proposed mission hospital at Chilonga, near Mpika, in the northern province. Earlier that year, 25 March, 1954, in a letter to the Bishop, she expressed a desire to visit Chilonga: "My intention is to go there just to see where the sisters would have to work."[4] In the same letter, she makes good her promise to send him "£6000 to build the convent with the help of God and His Holy Mother." She assures him that there are three nursing sisters about to begin their midwifery training, and they would be ready to begin work at the new hospital as soon as it was built

One is struck by Mother Antonia's enthusiasm regarding the first mission of the Congregation in Africa. This is evident in all her correspondence with Bishop Van den Biesen. At the age of 65, and wearing the black serge habit of pre-Vatican II, her energy and intense interest in the new venture are apparent. Her thoughts and remarks are those of a visionary who saw a great future of apostolic work among the most needy. Yet, her feet were firmly on the ground as she made that pioneering journey with her Assistant, Mother Adrienne Harkin. On leaving London, 6 September, 1954, she noticed 'the startling headline' on the newspaper of the passenger sitting in front of her, giving

> the story of the unfortunate air tragedy at Shannon the previous day. There was a look of anxiety on many faces on the plane, but we were in God's Hands and on our way to blaze the trail for Him in Africa.[5]

As Mother Antonia noted, the flight from London to Nairobi took the two sisters and the thirty-six passengers southwards over the snow-covered Alps, Rome, the Bay of Naples, Cairo, the endless Sahara Desert, Ethiopia, Khartoum and finally Nairobi. This was the stopping-off place before the last leg of the journey to Northern Rhodesia. There were three stops en route, at Rome, Cairo and Khartoum, mainly due to problems "with the electricity'.[6]

Chapter 1 – Blazing the Trail

In Nairobi, the sisters were given their first introduction to Africa by Fathers John and Martin Reidy, brothers of Sr. Vincienne. Even by 1954 standards, Nairobi seemed a progressive city with banks, schools and churches. The surrounding hilly country was well-cultivated with terraced plantations of coffee, tea, maize, bananas and citrus fruits. Mother Antonia was fascinated by the African people and was particularly impressed by the courtesy of the men who waited on the Sisters at table. She admired the mothers "carrying their babies on their backs". She observed how hard they worked: "The poor women seem to be doing all the work – carrying wood on their heads."[7]

She admits that she became so interested in the African people that she

> completely forgot that it was Friday and took bacon for breakfast. We had great fun about it afterwards when I discovered my mistake.[8]

In her letter, Mother Antonia refers to the gap between the rich white settlers – one per cent of the population – and the poor Africans. She took note of "the beautiful private houses" and added that she wondered "what those wealthy people were doing there".'[9] At the time of her visit, Kenya was undergoing one of the greatest political upheavals in its history, which took place from 1952 until 1958, when the country, under the leadership of Jomo Kenyatta, fought for independence from the Imperial British Government.

It was 10 September, 1954, and continuing their journey towards their final destination, the Sisters took the plane from Nairobi to the small airport at Abercorn, on the southern tip of Lake Tanganika. The flight took them over Tanzania and the Rift Valley of East Africa. On the approach to Northern Rhodesia, the vast expanse of bush vegetation gave way to a green, dense forest which contrasted with the arid deserts of the north. To herald the summer rains in October – the hottest month – the forests produced a sweet scent that assured the people that the growing season was not far away. Disembarking at Abercorn Airport, the Sisters must have felt for the first time the oppressive summer heat of Central Africa.

On arriving at Abercorn, Mother Antonia describes the person who met them as

> "a well-dressed gentleman in white who came towards us and my first impression was that he was some very important official as he appeared to be wearing a chain of office. I had never seen a White Father's habit, but when he came closer to us I could see it was a Rosary round his neck."[10]

His name was Father Pelletier and, having welcomed them, he handed Mother Antonia a letter from Father Boenders, the Vicar Delegate, and assured her he was only an "ordinary White Father from French Canada".[11] After signing the necessary immigration documents, witnessed by a British Police Chief, the Sisters were on their way to the remote parts of the country.

They were driven southwards by Father Pelletier along a hazardous dirt road to the White Fathers' Mission at Mwanbe-Mwela, close to the Tanzanian border. This was a significant place to begin since Mambwe-Mweta is considered the first Catholic Mission in the country.

> In August 1891, Missionaries of Africa, popularly known as the White Fathers because of their white robes, settled in Mambwe-Mwela in the far north, and from there they founded a string of mission posts among the Bemba.[12]

Chapter 1 – Blazing the Trail

Mother Antonia gave her first impression of the place when she commented: "There we saw poverty in the extreme." She greatly appreciated the White Fathers' hospitality during her overnight stay, especially in giving her

> the bishop's room, with a little narrow camp bed, no room to turn in it, an orange box for a washstand, a little enamel jug and basin and a whiskey bottle for drinking water.[13]

She added: "Mother Adrienne's room was not as good as mine".

Early next morning, the Sisters were on the road again, driving 170 miles to llondola Cathedral for the ordination of two African Deacons. They were accompanied by the mother of one of the deacons, who belonged to the White Fathers' Mission at Mambwe. There was great excitement among the local people, as Mother Antonia recorded:

> The whole village turned out to see us all off, and the cries of the little children were pitiable when they saw their mother going away.[14]

The mother had lost her husband a month previously, and the Sisters were not happy that "she had the worst seat in the car, the men always took the best places."[15]

The ordination of two African priests was a big event in the lives of the people of Northern Rhodesia. As Mother Antonia pointed out in her letter: "This ceremony was unique, Africans ordained by an African Bishop."[16] The Bishop's name was Bishop Rugambwa of the Rulado Prefecture. The year was 1954 and the fact that this part of Africa had its own clergy at this point in time is no small tribute to the White Fathers and the other missionaries who had been evangelising there since the 1890s.

At Ilondola, the Sisters were grateful for the warm hospitality of the White Sisters, who were regarded as 'saints' by Mother Antonia. They taught in the schools and their German Superior had spent many years in Rhodesia. The ordination ceremony was followed by a lively entertainment from the seminarians and a buffet lunch. Among the guests were the British District Commissioner and the local chief,

> a pagan with six wives, one in each village. He gave a speech and thanked God for the graces bestowed on Africa that day.[17]

Under the Federal Government of Rhodesia and Nyasaland, the establishment of a mission hospital necessitated approval from various authorities. Among those who had to be consulted were the Governor General, the District Commissioner and the Chief and Provincial Medical Officers. At that time, these posts were held mostly by British citizens. Bishop Van den Biesen had many anxious moments trying to obtain the final go-ahead for the hospital and the accompanying grants. In March, 1954, he wrote to Mother Antonia:

> I am confident, however, that they [the Government] will help us with fifty per cent of the cost of the hospital buildings and grants for staff.[18]

An added problem for the Bishop was the long delay awaiting a reply from the Government

> because of the muddle they are in from rearranging the Government machinery under the recent Federation. Then of course will come the lengthy procedure of a demo-

cratic government and our demands will have to pass one commission after another before they are finally agreed upon.[19]

However, he advised Mother Antonia:

> You should not be disturbed by our financial difficulties. This is the daily bread of almost every missionary bishop, lack of funds and lack of personnel.[20]

In her reply to his letter, she reminds him that "Prayer can move mountains, so we must get down to storming Heaven for Chilonga."[21]

To discuss future plans for the hospital, Mother Antonia's next stop was a visit to the Provincial Medical Officer at Mulinansolo in the Northern Province. The meeting was cordial and the gentleman was a Catholic Pole "with whom we discussed the future hospital as far as we could."[22]

Not far away, at Kasama Hospital, the Sisters had their first encounter with victims of leprosy and smallpox patients. The matron, who was from Cheshire, made a great impression on Mother Antonia and she wrote: "I don't know how she is able to cope with it all"[23] On the same day, the Sisters arrived at their destination, Chilonga, the place where Bishop Van den Biesen had chosen for the mission hospital. The car journey of 150 miles from Kasama took them along a dirt road through the sparsely populated region of the northern province, through the swamps of the Chambezi river, as far as the foothills of the Muchinga Escarpment, where one of the White Fathers' oldest missions (1899) was situated. Mother Antonia admired the beautiful mission church where they prayed and attended Mass with the White Fathers. She described them as "German,

English speaking and very kindly". She was happy to write that she and Mother Adrienne had "selected the site for the hospital" which was to be the Congregation's first mission in Africa.[24] The site for the convent was close by, in a picturesque setting with the escarpment rising steeply above it. Bishop Van den Biesen's choice of location for Chilonga Hospital was far-sighted. Not only would it meet the medical needs of the District of Mpika, but it would also serve as a haven for the many weary travellers along the Great North Road (from the Cape in South Africa to Cairo) in the years ahead.

Mother Antonia's next appointment was with the Chief Medical Officer in Lusaka, the capital city, almost 400 miles from Chilonga. In the 1950s, this was still a small town linked to Southern Rhodesia and South Africa by a good road and railway. Similarly to the north a tarmac road and a railway led to the Copperbelt towns of Ndola, Kitwe and Chingola. En route to Lusaka, the Sisters stayed overnight with the Dominican Sisters at Broken Hill (now Kabwe), at that time a thriving mining town. Here they joined the good road to Lusaka, a welcome change from the red dust and uneven surfaces of the bush roads. Mother Antonia pays tribute to the two White Fathers who "took turns at the wheel", driving over 800 miles from Abercorn to Lusaka, often in challenging road conditions.

The meeting with the Head of the Medical Board, Dr. Evans, was a pleasant experience. He treated the Sisters "with great courtesy and agreed to pay fifty per cent of the cost of the hospital and convent."[25] He suggested two other places where he thought there was a great need for hospitals, but Mother Antonia thought it best to await the Bishop's final decision. Accompanying the Sisters to the Medical Board was Father Killian Flynn OFM.Cap.[26] He was competent to advise Mother

Antonia on educational and medical matters. He seems to have worked a minor miracle in securing two seats on a plane to Nairobi for the return flight to London.

After an absence of eighteen days from the Mother House, Chigwell, U.K., Mother Antonia received her first cable from the Sisters telling her that all was well. Before departing from Nairobi, she made a final visit to a hospital. Here she was moved to pity when she saw patients "who had only a mat on the bed and one blanket over them."[27] She ends this circular letter with a description of "the injured Mau Mau prisoners guarded by the military,"[28] who suffered from atrocities committed by their captors during the Mau Mau uprising.[29]

Mother Antonia's pioneering visit to this underdeveloped part of Central Africa was accomplished. Now she had seen for herself the places where the sisters would have to work. Despite the difficulties, some of them apparently insurmountable, she was undeterred, and already she had the names of those sisters who would be pioneers in the new mission hospital. She had indeed "blazed the trail"!

NOTES

1. Phillips, Rev. Mother Antonia. *Circular Letter to the Sisters of the Congregation*, Zambia: Sept., 1954. (Future references to Rev. Mother Antonia's letters will appear as R.M.A.)

    Reverend Mother Antonia. Born Mary J. Phillips at Kilmuckridge, Co. Wexford, 25 May, 1889. Entered the Congregation at Chigwell, 28 May, 1909. Professed 28 Aug., 1911. Died at Kelton, 17 Jan. 1974. Superior General 1941-1963. Awarded O.B.E by Queen Elizabeth II, 1956.

2. Originally Servants of the Sacred Heart, founded in Versailles, 1866, by Father Victor Braun. The Congregation became independent in 1903 under the name of Sisters of the Sacred Hearts of Jesus and Mary.

3. Van den Biesen, Bishop Joseph. Born at Breda, Netherlands, 16 April, 1913. Vicar Apostolic of Abercorn 1951-1958. Died 4 March, 2001.

    At the time of the visit. Bishop Van den Biesen was on a fund-raising tour of America.

4. R.M.A. *Letter to Bishop Vanden Biesen*, Chigwell. 25th March, 1954.

5-9. R.M.A. op. cit.

10. White Fathers so named because of the white cassocks and red fezzes which they originally wore. Founded by Cardinal Lavigerie (1825-1892), Archbishop of Carthage and Algiers, Primate of Africa. Crusaded against the Slave Trade for which he founded an order of priests in 1868 called Missionaries of Africa, known as White Fathers. Founded a similar order of Brothers and Nuns. Died in Algiers, 26 Nov. 1892.
    Sollier, J.F. "Charles-Martial-Allemand Lavigerie." *Catholic Encyclopedia*, New York: Robert Appleton Company; 1913.

11. R.M.A. opcit.

12. Hinfelaar, H.F. M.Afr. *History of the Catholic Church in Zambia: 1895-1995*. Lusaka: Bookworld Publishers, 2004. p. 1.

13-17. R.M.A. op. cit.

18-20. Van den Biesen, Bishop Joseph. *Letter to Mother Antonia*, Zambia: March, 1954.

21-25. R.M.A. op. cit.

26. Hinfelaar, H. F. op. cit. p. 286. "Fr. Killian Flynn O.F.M. Cap. Worked as a pioneer missionary in Zambia from 1931 to 1972, when he left for Nairobi. He founded the Catholic Secretariat in Zambia in 1960. He died 3rd December, 1972."

27, 28. R.M.A. op. cit.

29. *The Guardian, Leader Comment*, "Kenya. Evil and the Empire", London: 6 May, 2013.

CHAPTER TWO

Preparing the Way

BY THE 1950S the political map of Africa was beginning to change. In 1960, the British Prime Minister, Harold MacMillan, declared to the South African Parliament:

> "The wind of change is blowing through this continent, and whether we like it or not, this growth of national consciousness is a political fact. We must all accept it as a fact, and our national policies must take account of it." [1]

To many missionaries, decolonisation seemed a long way off but time proved them wrong. In 1929, Northern Rhodesia came under Indirect Rule from Britain.

> But after the imposition of the Federation of Northern and Southern Rhodesia and Nyasaland in 1953, change was in the air. It was manifested in strikes among students at Chikuni, a Jesuit College, and other secondary schools.[2]

Catholic missionaries were often criticised for having "too comfortable a co-existence with the administration of the colonial regime,"[3] but the Church authorities realised that open confrontation with the political administration would impede the pace of progress in education and health care provision in the country. Even today, the many hospitals, schools, colleges and training centres established in the 1940s and 50s continue the services for which they were founded.

It was in this environment that the Sisters of the Sacred Hearts of Jesus and Mary began their ministry to the poor and sick in Northern Rhodesia. Despite Bishop Van den Biesen's predictions about the slow-moving pace of Government Departments, events seem to happen sooner than expected. In August, 1955, he wrote to Mother Antonia:

> Everything is going according to plan. The latest proposals by the Federal Ministry of Health regarding Mission Hospitals are almost certain to go through, because they are already in force in both Southern Rhodesai and Nyasaland, i.e. the biggest part of the Federation.[4]

Throughout 1955, the Bishop was engaged in intensive activity, drawing up plans for the hospital buildings and forming a contract acceptable to the Congregation and to the Government's Director of Medical Services. From his residence in Abercorn, he made frequent trips of 600 miles along dangerous roads to Lusaka, via Chilonga, to secure approval of plans and proposals. He was happy to report to Mother Antonia that the hospital plans had been approved and regarded as 'excellent'. He added: "Much careful thought was given to their drawing up. Initial grants are already coming forward."[5] Work on the hospital was going well. The water scheme was now operational. It seemed that all would be ready by April or May 1956, and the pioneer Sisters were expected to start work in June.

Mother Antonia received a draft copy of the Government Contract in August 1955. The Bishop invited her to make any comments or changes she deemed necessary. He told her:

> I have given it long and careful consideration, trying to be as reasonable as possible, and to give the Sisters and Doctor as much freedom of action as I think I could give.[6]

The Contract was duly signed by Mother Antonia, the Bishop and the Director of Medical Services, Lusaka. The agreement was valid for ten years and it obliged the Congregation to provide trained nursing staff (State Registered Nurses and Midwives). The number would be reviewed from time to time. The Sisters would also be responsible for training African nurses. The religious rights of the Congregation would be protected, and ministers of any religion would be allowed to minister to patients. Salaries, leave and other conditions of service would be the same as those of similarly qualified staff employed by the Government. The Senior Sister of the Nursing Staff would be recognised as the Sister-in-Charge of the staff and of the general activities of the hospital under the direction of the Director, his Medical Staff and the Matron-in-Chief.[7]

As already discussed in Chapter 1, Mother Antonia had named the three 'pioneers' after her first visit to Africa. They were: Sister Kieran Marie, Sister Mary La Salette and Sr. Mary of the Sacred Heart. They had volunteered for the African foundation and were highly motivated for their mission to spread the Faith by the testimony of their lives, dedicated to serving the poor and sick, especially mothers and children. In the course of his pastoral ministry, Bishop Van den Biesen had seen the great need of care for women in childbirth, and he was emphatic that each Sister should have a midwifery qualification. Infant mortality was much higher in the 1950s than it is today. The deaths of young mothers were preventable with good medical care.

When arranging for Residents' Permits for the Sisters, Mother Antonia corresponded with Mr. W. H. Lowe, Secretary to the British Immigrants' Selection Board at Rhodesia House, in the Strand, London. Once their application forms were signed, she did not hesitate to request financial help from him towards their travelling expenses by sea. It was decided that their journey would be by ship to enable them to take large termite-proof trunks carrying essentials for the new hospital. A six months orientation course in the country was planned for the Sisters before they began their work at the hospital in Chilonga. This would enable them to learn the Bemba language and help them to reach out to the people of the Northern Province. During this time, the White Sisters,[8] who were experienced missionaries, would accommodate them in their convent at Chilubula and initiate them into their new missionary way of life.

Missionaries are no strangers to setbacks and disappointments. Three months before the proposed date of departure, 9 February, 1956, Sister La Salette became ill and had to be hospitalised. Her travel ticket was cancelled and re-booked for a later date. This was a great disappointment for her and her two companions. During the previous months, they had been making preparations together for their distant mission by attending courses in radiography, pharmacy, and also taking driving lessons. Bishop Van den Biesen had congratulated them on passing their medical examinations in midwifery and in tropical medicine, and, characteristically thinking ahead of the needs of the Chilonga Mission, he wondered

> whether one of the Sisters could do a course in Dentistry. This would be extremely useful in helping people, even Fathers, instead of having to go as far as Broken Hill or Ndola.[9]

Chapter 2 – Preparing the Way

Before the 1950s, it was uncommon for Religious women to drive motor vehicles. For Sisters on the missions it was essential. Even a high level of driving competence at home was insufficient preparation for the potholes and mudslides of the African dirt roads, and the Sisters could find themselves at the wheel of cars, vans, ambulances and sometimes even tractors!

Shortly before the departure of the Sisters from Chigwell, Bishop Van den Biesen wrote to Mother Antonia:

> I am delighted to hear of the departure of the Sisters. To make everything more watertight, I am forwarding here the documentary evidence of employment as under No. 6 of the Notes on Instructions of Application Forms for entering the Federation. I shall come personally to receive the Reverend Sisters at Lusaka. I could then present them to the Director of Medical Services before we disappear into the bush![10]

The second phase of the new foundation in Zambia had now been accomplished. Everything was ready for the Sisters to commence the missionary work so dear to Mother Antonia' heart.

NOTES
1. Macmillan, Rt. Hon. H. *Speech to the Parliament of South Africa*. Pretoria: Feb. 1960.
2. Hinfelaar, H.F. *History of the Catholic Church in Zambia: 1895-1995*. Lusaka: Bookworld Publishers, 2004. p. 167.
3-6. Van den Biesen, Bishop Joseph. *Letter to Mother Antonia*, Zambia: Aug. 1955.
7. *Medical Services*, Lusaka; 1955.
8. Missionaries of Africa, known as White Sisters. See Chap. 1, Notes 5-10.
9-10. Van den Biesen, Bishop Joseph, op. cit.

CHAPTER 3

Making History

SISTER KIERAN MARIE and Sister Mary of the Sacred Heart left Chigwell Convent on 9 February, 1956. This was a momentous occasion in the history of the Congregation, although it was not without a sense of sadness. There was also a concern that owing to the remoteness of this mission the Sisters might experience a sense of isolation from the main Congregation in the U.K. The histories of many Religious Orders attest to how easily this can happen. Home visits were rare and infrequent in those days. Despite rapid development in aviation, letters could take several weeks to reach Central Africa. With the exception of a few towns, there were no telephone links with the rest of the world.

In her first Circular Letter, 14 February, 1956, after the Sisters had left for Northern Rhodesia, Mother Antonia caught the mood of the occasion. She began by describing the ceremony on the eve of their departure:

> Our dear Sisters have departed for our Congregation's first foundation in Africa. Our new Bishop, (Bishop Beck of Brentwood) very graciously came to address the Pioneers, giving them his Episcopal mission or sending forth in the

Chapter 3 – Making History

parting words of Our Lord: "Go out into the highways and hedges and compel them to come in that my House may be full." After the address, the Sisters approached the altar steps and kneeling, received his blessing and a scroll bearing the blessing of our Holy Father, Pope Pius XII, which the Bishop handed to Mother Kieran Marie.[1]

That evening the first evening Mass was celebrated in Chigwell Convent as part of a parish mission. "It was," as Mother Antonia regarded it, "a fitting preparation for the Sisters' leave-taking the following morning." All lights were extinguished except on the sanctuary so that all could focus on the Eucharist Celebration. "Sister Columbanus played the organ by the light of a hand torch – all most impressive."[2]

From her account of the Sisters' departure the following morning, one can sense Mother Antonia's sadness as if she felt personal responsibility for this mission:

> As you can well imagine, there was a solemn hush, as we did not trust ourselves to speak our feelings. Quietly the travellers got into the car, myself, Mother Bernadette, Mother Redempta, Mother Kieran Marie and Sister Mary of the Sacred Heart. Snow was falling fast as the white-veiled novices lined the driveway. The professed Sisters gathered round the paths, the staff were in groups here and there, handkerchiefs waved and they were gone![3]

The 'Pioneers' travelled to Waterloo Station in London to take the boat train to Southampton where they would board the 'Athlone Castle' liner to Cape Town. At Waterloo there were farewells from the Sisters at Hillington, Leyton, Lewisham, Mile-End, Dagenham and Homerton. Redemptorist Fathers from Clapham were also there, seeing off Father Freeman

C.S.S.R. who was travelling to South Africa. His presence was a welcome surprise as it meant that daily Mass could be celebrated during the voyage.

At Southampton, Mother Antonia and her companions boarded the 'Athlone Castle' and inspected the cabin which would be the living quarters for the Sisters during the next two weeks. She was happy that it was 'comfortable' and expressed her delight that "Sister Mary of the Sacred Heart was able to phone her mother from the state room of the liner."[4] In her account of the final farewell, Mother Antonia did not hide her feelings as she conveyed her sense of loss and separation:

> At 3.30 pm the big bell warned all non-passengers off. We stood beside the boat near enough to speak to them and bid a last farewell. At 4.00 pm sharp the 'Athlone Castle' moved quietly from the dock, the Sisters standing very bravely at the deck-rail, smiling and waving. The space widened, speed gathered, we remained there till the dear ones were lost to view.[5]

The long and quite arduous journey that lay ahead is described by Sister Mary of the Sacred Heart who dutifully kept a Journal from the time they embarked at Southampton, 9 February 1956, until their arrival in Cape Town, 2 March, and after that an account of the three-day train journey from the Cape to Lusaka in Northern Rhodesia. For both Sisters, the assignment to the new mission in Central Africa was a life-changing experience. Sister Kieran Marie was appointed the Sister-in-Charge. She was 46 years of age and was a nurse and midwife with considerable administrative skills. Her faith was strong and she was a natural optimist. She was also blessed with boundless energy and was not afraid to take initiatives. Sister Mary of the Sacred Heart, 27 years of age and younger in religious life and in nursing experience, enjoyed meeting a challenge. She saw her vocation as a privileged means of bringing the healing power of Christ to the people of Africa. On the first night of the sea voyage she recorded:

> We went back to our cabin, somewhat unsteadily, as the sea was very rough. We said our night prayers, including Evening Office, then to bed feeling very happy, even though we missed all the Sisters.[6]

Sailing into the choppy waters of the Bay of Biscay led to the expected rolling and swaying of the ship. Anti-seasick medication helped towards preventing sickness throughout the voyage. The Sisters remembered the feasts of Sister Scholastica, 10 February, and Sister Marie de Lourdes on the 11th. Many humorous situations are recorded, for example:

> The steward who served us on the first day informed us this afternoon that he mustn't be well with God as he prayed we would be at his table. He came over to ask how the Sisters of Mercy were. We told him we weren't Sisters of Mercy. He said it did not matter as we were all on the same mission![7]

A pleasant break in the sea voyage came when the 'Athlone Castle' called to the port of Las Palmas in the Canary Islands, 13 February. Although the stopping-off time was only three hours, the Sisters and Father Freeman were able to go ashore to celebrate Mass in the Cathedral. They enjoyed the taxi ride in "an old lime-green Ford as the driver hooted in and out of brightly-lit bazaars" where visitors were treated to a barrage of market sellers cheerily holding up their wares to encourage buyers. All this was a welcome diversion from sailing on the high seas. Before re-embarking, they were taken to the Catholic

Church of Saint Catherine, where Christopher Columbus is said to have prayed before his historic visit to North America.[8]

On Ash Wednesday, 14 February, Mass was celebrated on board the ship, but without ashes and with a noticeable increase in the size of the congregation. The temperatures began to rise as they sailed further south into the tropics and it was time to change into white habits. "This was a relief but how to keep them clean was another question!"[9]

On 11 February, the Sisters made the acquaintance of a Mr. Neville from Rochdale, Sister Mary's home town, who was returning to Ndola having been on home leave. The encounter was not a cheerful one. Although he had high praise for the White Fathers in Ndola and the Dominican Sisters who taught his daughter, he was ungenerous in his comments about the African people. Sister Mary wrote:

> He sympathised with us who are going to be with them so much. I am afraid he did not give us any encouragement at all, not that it matters very much.[10]

Over a week into the voyage, with temperatures rising rapidly, the passengers caught sight of land off the coast of Liberia. The monotony of the sea voyage was broken as the ship entered equatorial waters and lively activities on deck provided exciting entertainment. There were no signs that the Sisters' enthusiasm ever flagged. They enjoyed a tour of the ship and the children's fancy dress parties. An adult sport, "The Tone Trial", provoked great fun:

> Six men did up ladies' hair in any style chosen by the men, all assembled with buckets of water and combs, and then the fun began. The poor ladies, I'm sure, were very sorry they had volunteered. There were prizes for the best re-

sults. One lady had a bottle of meltonian cream spread all over her hair, and then a little sailor doll was placed on top to represent the surf and the sailor. She certainly deserved the first prize.[11]

Temperatures began to drop slowly as the 'Athlone Castle' entered cooler waters south of the Tropic of Capricorn. On 20 February, passengers were eagerly awaiting their first glimpse of the Cape of Good Hope, "some for the first time like ourselves and some people returning after leave."[12]

On 22 February, the ship took the full force of the violent south-easterly winds, the nightmare of sailors in former times. Sister Mary recorded:

> We have come into the 'Cape Rollers' as the big waves near the Cape are called. The sea is rough and similar to what it was in the Bay of Biscay. While I'm writing this, a boy student is chasing his study books up and down the table as they slide when the ship lurches.[13]

Sailing into Cape Harbour was unforgettable as the illuminated Table Mountain came into view. The liner had travelled 5975 miles from Southampton and now the end was in sight. Daylight came quickly at 5.30 am as the 348 passengers sang South African songs from the deck. Both Sisters were speedily cleared by Immigration officials. When the Post Office Authorities came on board, they sent off telegrams to the Mother House in Chigwell and to their families. Unexpectedly, they were met by Brother Martin, Superior of the Christian Brothers, and by Brother Carthage, a brother of Sister Mary David O'Farrell. Sister Mary wrote:

> We presume that it was through Sister David they knew we were arriving in Cape Town. They were both very kind to us, they knew the ropes and everyone knew them![14]

At the Customs' shed, the two Brothers helped by arranging with Cook's Travel for the transfer of the trunks and cases to the railway station for departure to Northern Rhodesia on Saturday, 25 February. The Sisters spent the intervening days with the Pallotine Sisters who directed a large hospital in Cape Town. Rev. Mother Etheltrudis gave them a warm and unforgettable welcome to Africa. Sister Mary's cousin, John, took them on a tour of the city, showing them breath-taking views of Table Mountain and Signal Hill. For the first time, they encountered the ugly face of apartheid. In the shops, banks and post offices there were separate counters for black and white people. Sister Mary remarked in her Journal:

> African people are dressed in rags and do all the menial work. Their poverty is extreme. However, we were to see much worse later on.[15]

The two Sisters were now on the last stage of their journey to the Mission which would be their home for many years to come. They could not foresee the many difficulties and trials which were awaiting them but their deep faith, fortitude and missionary zeal provided them with a solid foundation to fulfil the Gospel message: "Go, then, to all peoples everywhere and make them my disciples… and I will be with you always to the end of time."[16]

NOTES

1-4.	R.M.A. *Circular Letter to the Congregation.* Chigwell: 14 Feb. 1956.
5-15.	McManus, Sister Maiy of the Sacred Heart, *Journal,* London-Cape Town: 9 Feb. – 22 Mar. 1956.
16.	*Gospel of St. Matthew* 27: vs. 19-20.

CHAPTER 4

Into Africa

THE TRAIN JOURNEY FROM CAPE TOWN to Northern Rhodesia took three days. Writing in her diary, Sr. Mary of the Sacred Heart gives an account of the route into Africa's interior that is full of endless variety and surprises. The train left the Cape at 2.00 pm. 25 February. Within their small 'coupe' or compartment, about seven feet by three feet, the Sisters organised their luggage and themselves, piling their cases on their beds during the day and stacking them in the limited space at night. Sr. Mary of the Sacred Heart saw the funny side of it all:

> The fun started when I had to get up to my bed, there were no footholds so I had to jump up and hope for the best![1]

They were attended by a cheerful steward who came from Ballintemple, Co. Cork. Meals were substantial, and, although different from what they were accustomed to, were quite tasty. African pumpkin seemed to be served at all the meals.

Journeying northwards, the Sisters left behind the lowlands of the Cape for the spectacular scenery of the Great Karoo mountains. For the first time, they saw the magnificence of the African continent as the train snaked its way across the Vaal River Valley, then into the endless Kalahari Desert. The train stopped at many stations en route and Sister Mary of the Sacred Heart records their first real encounter with the African people:

> People run from all directions, some selling ornaments, such as carved elephants, or lions, or even walking sticks. There are lots and lots of children and cripples too at the train stations. They go along from window to window with their hands held out begging for anything you could give them. They are so pitifully thin and dressed in rags. There is not a fat child among them. Indeed their little legs are so thin one would wonder how they manage to support their little bodies. But for all that they are extremely courteous and know how to say 'thank you' in English. We found our surplus food and fruit much appreciated.[2]

Coming into Southern Rhodesia (Zimbabwe) the landscape became greener and more dense. There were more frequent signs of human habitation situated dangerously close to the railway line. "The people waved and shouted from the oldest to the youngest."[3] With Bulawayo only a few hours away, the Rhodesian Custom Officials boarded the train, going into every compartment. All went well for the Sisters. At Bulawayo they changed trains for Northern Rhodesia. Before moving on, they were welcomed by the Franciscan Sisters of the Divine Motherhood (Guildford, U.K.) who provided them with lunch and helped them to transfer their luggage. The diary records:

> We pulled out of Bulawayo and left Mother Dominic and the Sisters who assured us we would love Africa. Then we settled down for the night, thankful to be on the last lap of the train journey at last.[4]

At 8 o'clock the following morning, 28 February, 1956, the train slackened speed so that the passengers would have a good view of the Victoria Falls on the mighty Zambezi River. From the gigantic railway bridge the view is magnificent, despite the thick misty spray that constantly hangs over the scene. The train came to a halt at the nearby town of Livingstone, named after the great explorer, Dr. David Livingstone. Without being aware of it, the Sisters were following roughly the same direction he took when penetrating Central Africa one hundred years previously. One of his greatest geographical discoveries was the Victoria Falls in 1855. At Livingstone, the Sisters were treated to more Franciscan hospitality by the order who ran the hospital there. Father Albert OFM Cap. took them to the Church of St. Therese of Lisieux for Mass.

Having crossed the Zambezi Gorge, the train entered what was then known as Northern Rhodesia, an emerging African nation. Lusaka, the country's capital, was now about three hundred miles away. The last part of the train journey would take the Sisters through the Southern Province which had considerable agricultural development along the railway line. But, as Sister Mary of the Sacred Heart recorded, "the poverty-stricken huts and villages"[5] were never far away. They saw a large herd of goats which appeared "fairly well nourished".[6] Along this route, a string of Catholic Missions was established. The Irish Jesuit Fathers were pioneers in the field of education and had successful schools at Chikuni and Monze. Well-run hospitals were set up by the Holy Rosary and Franciscan Sisters to meet the medical needs of the people of the Southern Province. Sister Kieran Marie and Sister Mary of the Sacred Heart looked forward to participating in the new nation's health care system.

Chapter 4 – Into Africa

Kafue, the railway station before Lusaka, is well-known for its National Park. Here the Sisters learnt that their train was almost three hours behind schedule and wondered what Bishop Van den Biesen would say about his long wait for their arrival. They forgot that he knew Africa better than they did! Sister Mary of the Sacred Heart wrote:

> At 10.40 pm. we could see the brightly coloured lights of Lusaka in the distance, and it was exactly 10.45 when we arrived, the end of a long three-day train journey.[7]

It was impossible to find the Bishop in the dimly-lit Lusaka railway station. As they paced up and down alongside the very long train, they could not see anyone resembling a cleric. Eventually, the Bishop, wearing a light blue jacket, found them. He was accompanied by an official from the Ministry of Health in Lusaka. They both gave the Sisters a hearty welcome and thanked them for coming to Northern Rhodesia. When the Bishop saw the amount of luggage they had brought with them, he remarked: "It looks as if you have come to stay, Sisters!"[8] The trunks were left at the station and the Bishop arranged to have them sent to Chilubula by road. The suitcases fitted into his "very big American car"[9] in which he would drive the Sisters to their destination six hundred miles away.

The first night in Lusaka was spent at the Dominican girls' school at Woodlands. The Sisters here were well-known for their hospitality towards missionaries in transit.

Next morning they met Father Killian Flynn OFM Cap, who represented the Catholic Missions at the Ministries of Health and Education. He gave them a great welcome, and Sr. Mary of the Sacred Heart described him as "a very fine priest".[10] Their next meeting was with the Medical Officer of Health, Dr.

Harrison, a non-Catholic Irishman, who received them graciously and gave them encouragement for the work they were about to undertake. "He promised his support at all times".[11]

Whilst still in Lusaka, the Sisters met Bishop (later Cardinal) Adam Kowlowiecki S.J. He had come from Poland in 1946 having spent the war years in concentration camps, mainly Dachau. In the years ahead, he was to play an important role in the new nation of Zambia.

The challenges the Sisters faced were brought home to them when they were given a tour of the African hospital in Lusaka. Sister Mary of the Sacred Heart wrote in her diary:

> Accompanied by Father Killian, Sister Kieran Marie and I had many shocks during this tour. The general impression was that anything was good enough for the Africans. The hospital had been built for 120 patients but they had 420 there. Beds were pushed up against one another and the patients looked miserable.[12]

The hospital chaplain, an Irish priest, Father Walsh S.J. (later chief advisor to President Kaunda) was an outstanding pastor who strove to meet the needs of the patients. European doctors and a 'very nice Scottish matron'[13] ran the hospital as best they could under such dire conditions.

Whilst still at the hospital, Father Killian gave the Sisters a 'little advice', as recounted in the diary:

> He said we should be very patient with the Africans and with ourselves. It would take some time to settle down, particularly as we were not with one of our own communities, and that we were not to get discouraged if we felt loneliness. We were to place our whole trust and Mission

> in Our Lord's Hands. We were only instruments which He would use when and how He pleased.
>
> Father said he was glad we both had a sense of humour as it is a great blessing on the missions. Most important would be the spirit of our first foundation and that it was very necessary for us to bring the spirit of our Congregation with us, and above all we were to try never to complain, especially when writing home, as the success of our mission would be won by our suffering and mortification, and our spirit.[14]

It was 1 March, 1956 when the two Sisters left for the last stretch of their four-hundred-mile journey into the bush – to Chilonga, their new foundation in the Northern Province. Before their departure, Fr. Killian blessed the car, laden with luggage, and added that with Bishop Van den Biesen's reputation for fast driving they would need extra protection! The journey retraced the one taken by Rev. Mother Antonia and Mother Adrienne the previous September. Their first stop was at Broken Hill (Kabwe) where again they received the customary Dominican hospitality. They continued northwards on the Great North Road until twilight at 6.30 pm. and then stopped for the night at the Mkushi River Hotel, run by Mr. and Mrs. Marshall from England. It was a surprise to find such a lovely place in the middle of the bush. Here they were waited on at table by African waiters dressed in white, with red sashes and red fezzes. They were very pleasant and courteous. At Mkushi, the Sisters had their first lesson in Chibemba, the language mainly spoken in the Northern Province. Sister Mary of the Sacred Heart wrote:

> The African people came to greet us clapping their hands and bending their knees saying "Mwapoleni", which

means "I hope you're well". The Bishop taught us to reply "Ndita Makwai" which means "I'm well. I hope you're well too."[15]

The travellers had another day's journey ahead of them when they left for Chilonga/Chilubula the following morning. They attended Mass at 6.00 am, for the intentions of Pope Pius XII. It was still the rainy season and the dirt road was muddy red and quite treacherous in some places. It stretched before them with miles and miles of dense forest on either side and not another vehicle in sight Bishop Van den Biesen maintained his record for driving at high speed, reaching up to 70-80 miles an hour, even after being beckoned by police to slow down! They reached the White Fathers' Mission at Serenje at 10.30 am. They were now in the Bishop's own diocese of Abercorn (Mbala), or Vicariate Apostolic as it was then named. (It became a diocese in 1959 under Bishop Furstenburg.) The Fathers and people at the Mission extended a warm welcome to the Sisters, who were treated to a large jug of home-brewed beer by the Catechist's wife.

Chilonga, their final destination, was less than a two-hour journey from Serenje. The Bishop continued with breath-taking speed, stopping only briefly to allow a zebra to cross the road as it emerged from the Luangwa Game Reserve. Along this route they saw the signpost to Chitambo Mission where Dr. Livingstone had died, 30 April, 1873, and where there is a plaque to his memory. Like other Christian missionaries, he saw his calling as one of alleviating the suffering of the African people.

The monotony of the Great North Road was broken when the Sisters caught sight of the White Fathers' Mission Church at Chilonga, where they arrived at 11.15 on the morning of 2

Chapter 4 – Into Africa

March, 1956. Driving up the long tree-lined avenue, they were reminded of the Chigwell Convent drive, still fresh in their memory. On their left they could see the newly built hospital, and to their right the beginnings of their future convent. From behind the trees, scores of children ran towards the car and surrounded it. Sister Mary of the Sacred Heart wrote:

> The Bishop had to stop. There were tiny tots and big boys and girls shouting "Mwapoleni!" The great volume of their voices certainly made itself heard. By this time, the Fathers at the Mission had heard the commotion and waited on the verandah wondering if we could get through.[16]

Five members of the White Fathers Order welcomed the Sisters as they entered the house. The first thing they noticed was a picture of Rev. Mother Antonia wearing the O.B.E. decoration recently awarded to her by Queen Elizabeth II. On the opposite wall hung a picture of Cardinal Lavigerie, the Founder of the White Fathers. On the verandah, the Sisters were formally welcomed with a song in Chibemba, translated by the Bishop. The schoolteachers told them that the pupils had been watching out for them for several days and everyone was happy that they were here at last.

In 1956, the missionaries were still working alongside the Colonial Administration and relations between them were usually good. The Sisters were often accommodated at the home of Mr. Fox, the District Commissioner at Mpika, fifteen miles from Chilonga. Mrs. Fox, who knew our Sisters in Harlow, was very pleased to welcome them. The D.C.'s house was used once a month as a Mass Centre for the people in the surrounding villages. At 6.30 am. next morning Bishop Van den Biesen began hearing Confessions and finished at 8.00 am. in time to celebrate Mass. Having seen the location of their future mission, the Sisters were ready to move on that afternoon to Chilubula, two hundred miles further north. Here their orientation would begin to prepare them for their new life on the African missions.

The remaining part of the journey took them into territory which had been evangelised by the White Fathers since the 1890s. The Church at Chilubula was one of their earliest missions and was consecrated by Bishop Joseph Dupont to Our Lady of Good Help, Queen of Africa. Bishop Dupont, a Frenchman, was a legendary missionary, who, against all odds, established missions in the virgin territory of Northern Rhodesia. Chilubula, where Bishop Dupont is buried, was therefore a fitting place to learn Chibemba and to become familiar with African ways and customs. The White Sisters were their mentors and teachers. They provided them with a comfortable environment and helped them to feel at home. Sr. Mary of the Sacred Heart described their new home:

> ...a cottage-type of house, with cement walls and a thatched roof made of grass. There is no ceiling. We look straight up at the grass. There are three rooms, hence the name 'Trinity House'.[17]

Their house was situated close to the White Sisters' Convent and the Girls' Training College, so the two Sisters did not feel isolated and gradually grew accustomed to a very different lifestyle. Sr. Mary of the Sacred Heart wrote in her diary:

> We have many things to get used to. Life is as different as it could be. There is no electricity or water supply. All the water is carried from the river by the girls. We have tilly lamps at night which draw all manner of insects.[18]

Chapter 4 – Into Africa

From Southampton, they had travelled a distance of 9,200 miles by sea, train and road. It was 3 March, 1956 when Sr. Mary of the Sacred Heart drew her long journal to a close:

> The Africans have a happy disposition. They sing their way through life. Sr. Kieran Marie and I are very happy here. We thank God for the privilege and opportunity to come and work for these dear people of His. There is so much to be done for them in every way, education, nursing, and anything else you could think of. Our part will be very small in comparison with what has yet to be done to help them. Thank God for willing that our dear Congregation should have a share in His missionfield.[19]

The first foundation in Africa of the Sisters of the Sacred Hearts of Jesus and Mary was now established. The rest of its history is like the grain of mustard seed in the Gospel parable – "the smallest of all seeds, but when it grows up it is the biggest of all plants."[20] The work of the Congregation was to expand and flourish, and the missionary spirit of our first missionaries enabled those who came after them to adapt to the many changes which took place in the Church and in Africa during the following years.

NOTES
1-9. McManus, Sister Mary of the Sacred Heart. *Journal*, Southampton-Cape Town: 25 Feb. 1956.
10. See Chapter 1, Note 26.
11-19. McManus, Sister Mary of the Sacred Heart. *Journal*, Cape Town-Chilubula: March, 1956.
20. Gospel of St. Mark; 4:30-32.

CHAPTER 5

'Ladies in White' – Getting Started

ONCE SISTERS KIERAN MARIE and Mary of the Sacred Heart had completed their six months orientation course, they were eager to begin the hospital ministry at Chilonga. They bade farewell to the White Sisters at Chilubula, expressing their gratitude to them for such an invaluable introduction to Africa. The time spent there had been a sound preparation for the challenges facing them in the years ahead. The language course in Chibemba, though basic, was sufficient to enable them to communicate with the local people. Several visits to the various missions in the Northern Province introduced them to a completely new way of life. The Church liturgies, too, were edifying. Describing the Holy Week Ceremonies at Ilondola Cathedral, Sr. Kieran Marie wrote:

> What a revelation it was! Between singing and clapping in the Bemba tradition, it took hours to complete the service. The people walk for miles to attend Mass which they only get every three months when the missionary priests can visit them in their remote villages.[1]

The first step towards preparing the hospital was to go on a shopping expedition to Ndola in the Copperbelt, a distance of

Chapter 5 – 'Ladies in White' – Getting Started

about six hundred miles from Chilubula. Sr. Kieran Marie described the experience:

> For this we were helped by Father Jack Robinson W.F. and his three-ton lorry which was not easy to climb into! He shortened the long journey by story-telling and singing songs. We arrived at the Dominican Convent in Ndola and received the warm hospitality of the Sisters there. We were able to collect fifty white beds and ten cots donated by Misereor, (a German secular aid agency). We saw this gift as our dream for Chilonga gradually coming true.[2]

The Sisters began their work at Chilonga Hospital on 24 September, 1956, the feast of Our Lady of Mercy. They were disappointed to find the hospital building unfinished and the convent far from ready for occupation. The building contractor engaged by Bishop Van den Biesen had disappeared.[3] Consequently, the administration block in the hospital was to be their home for many months. However, they were grateful for the new 'comforts' that awaited them, one being the gift of running water, a welcome change from having to draw it in buckets from a well. The hospital ministry really began on bicycles. The Sisters cycled around the villages making the acquaintance of the local people, who were a little apprehensive of the 'Ladies in White'. To reassure them, Fr. Rou W.F. told them that the Sisters had a lot of medical knowledge and that they had come to help them.[4]

Back at the Mother House in Chigwell, Mother Antonia was keen that that the new convent in Chilonga should be completed so that the Sisters could form a community. In this way, they would be able to resume the ordinary, everyday rhythm of their lives to which they had been accustomed at home. Sister La Salette's recovery from illness was remarkably quick and she was ready to take up her nursing assignment by October, 1956. Accompanying her on the long sea voyage was Sister Canice, whose mission was to organise the new convent, adapting it to the needs of the community. On 8 November, the Bishop wrote to Mother Antonia:

> You have already heard of the good journey of Sister La Salette and Sister Canice and their arrival at Chilonga where the entire community is now under one roof, even with a private chapel. When I saw them the last time the Sisters were all happy and healthy, and with God's help we may get the convent ready for Christmas. My visit was in the company of the Medical Officer at Kasama. He was very pleased and the Sisters served us a marvellous lunch, during which I could admire the beautiful crockery you sent from England... Thank you very much indeed for all you sent, helping us to save money from our poor Vicariate cash-box of which we constantly see the bottom![5]

Despite being surrounded by builders and lacking basic facilities such as electricity, the Sisters forged ahead as best they could. Soon, the hospital opened its doors to the sick. Expectant mothers were accommodated in the operating theatre until the labour ward was ready. Patients with all manner of illnesses presented themselves, especially with malaria, dysentery and malnutrition, to name a few. Generous donations of medicine had already arrived at the hospital from countries like West Germany and the U.S.A., and the Sisters were able to address many of their patients' ailments. Unfortunately, there was no resident doctor, but a visiting doctor from the Provincial Headquarters at Kasama came frequently to advise the Sisters and to perform urgent operations. From Sister La Salette's diary we have the following account of one such operation:

Brother Gottlieb W.F. (a German brother and one of the builders) suffered from a strangulated hernia and he implored the doctor to save his life. The doctor and Sisters took the risk, in spite of the fact that they had no electricity or sterilising equipment. Because ether is highly flammable the operation had to be performed by torchlight. Storm-lamps and candles were dangerous. The operation was a success and the patient recovered normally.[6]

Just one year after the pioneers departed from Chigwell, Bishop Van den Biesen wrote to Mother Antonia giving her an account of how the small community at Chilonga had adapted so rapidly to the hardships and privations of the missionary environment:

From Chilonga I only get good news and I am so pleased your dear Sisters adapt themselves so well to this country, and love to work for our poor people in and around Chilonga.[7]

If setting up the hospital was mostly an uphill effort, there were also times for enjoyment and relaxation, organised by the White Fathers and Brothers at the mission. Sister Kieran Marie wrote about the many occasions they visited beauty spots such as the Nachikulu Caves, the Tundulila Falls and the Luangwa Valley National Park which was teeming with wild life. The White Fathers provided the transport and the Sisters organised the picnics![8]

Support was also given to the Sisters by the colonial officials at the District Administrative Office (BOMA) at Mpika. They were readily available for advice when needed. Among the most remembered names of District Commissioners (D.Cs) are Robin Lindsay Stewart, Peter Moss and Jack Fairchild.

From the very beginning, it was Sister Kieran Marie's vision that once the hospital building was completed, the Sisters would establish a training school for young African nurses who would eventually take over the administration of the Chilonga Hospital. The approval of the Federal Government Medical Officer was necessary for this new venture, and it required the appointment of a permanent resident doctor. True to her missionary vocation, Sr. Kieran Marie started the necessary proceedings in order to realise her dream. However, it was not an easy path to follow, but the faith and endurance of the first missionary Sisters of the Sacred Hearts of Jesus and Mary would triumph over all adversity.

NOTES
1-3. Pilkington, Sr. Kieran Marie. *Letter to Mother Antonia*. Zambia: 1956.
4-5. Van den Biesen, Bishop Joseph. *Letter to Mother Antonia*, Zambia: Nov. 1956.
6. McCaw, Sr. La Salette. *Diary*, Zambia: Dec. 1956.
7. Van den Biesen, Bishop Joseph, op. cit.
8. Pilkington, Sr. Kieran Marie, op. cit.

CHAPTER 6

Historic Events

"If the Good God wants us there..."
(Mother Antonia)

THE YEAR 1957 was a milestone in the history of the Congregation of the Sacred Hearts of Jesus and Mary insofar as the first foundation had been made in mission territory. It was also a significant year for the Catholic Church in Africa. While Bishop Van den Biesen (6 Feb. 1957) and Mother Antonia (19 March, 1957) were exchanging letters regarding future foundations in Northern Rhodesia, Pope Pius XII was about to publish his *Encyclical, Fidei Donum* (Easter Sunday, 21st April, 1957), in which he addressed the Bishops of the entire Catholic Church. This encyclical referred to "the present conditions of the Catholic missions, especially in Africa".[1]

In *Fidei Donum*, the Holy Father expressed a sense of urgency and exhorted the Bishops "to support with zealous interest the most holy cause of bringing the Church of God to all the world".[2] He hoped that his admonitions would "arouse a keener interest in the missionary apostolate among priests and through them set the hearts of the faithful on fire".[3] With specific reference to Africa, Pope Pius told the Bishops:

> We deem it fitting at the present moment to direct your serious attention to Africa – the Africa that is at long last reaching out towards the higher civilisation of our times and aspiring to civil maturity, the Africa that is involved in such grave upheavals as perhaps have never been recorded in her ancient annals.[4]

Clearly Bishop Van den Biesen was in tune with Pope Pius XII's apostolic zeal. No sooner had he established the hospital at Chilonga than he set about making plans for a new secondary school for African girls in his Vicariate of Abercorn (Mbala) in the Northern Province. We have already observed his concern for the health care of African women, which was the raison d'etre for the Chilonga hospital. His next step was to have young girls educated to a level at which they could be trained to become future leaders in their own country. At this time (1957) there was only one secondary school for African girls in Northern Rhodesia. This was in the Southern Province, near Livingstone, and was directed by the Franciscan Sisters.

The Bishop considered the proposed school to be of the utmost importance. He could read the signs of the times very clearly, although he may not have been aware that Northern Rhodesia's independence was only six years away. With his characteristic zeal and enthusiasm, he began the difficult work of negotiating with the Federal Government to obtain the approval and grants to which mission schools were entitled. Providing staff for a mission school in Central Africa presented a major problem and once again he turned to Mother Antonia. Attached to a letter dated 6 Feb. 1957 was a detailed document setting out the qualifications required for secondary school teachers under the Federal Government of Rhodesia. Commenting on the document, he wrote:

You will see that they put the requirements of the Education department very high. I think they are right, because in a country like this where so much depends on how the actual youth is being trained it is very important that we give them the best possible education. If your Congregation could gradually send out this staff with the qualifications as indicated there is no doubt that it would be the top school in Northern Rhodesia, and that's what we really want.[5]

During this period in post-war Britain, there was a huge increase in the child population leading to a pressing demand for more schools and teachers. The need was great in the Catholic school sector, which required more and more members of Religious Orders to train as teachers in order to staff the ever-growing number of Catholic schools. This was also a time of phenomenal growth in religious vocations which resulted in the capacity of Religious Orders to extend their ministries to other parts of the world. In 1953, under Mother Antonia's leadership, a group of five teaching Sisters had been sent to the Diocese of Fresno, in California. It was no surprise, then, that Mother Antonia informed the Bishop that she very much regretted not being able to spare any more teaching Sisters, adding: "We are very interested in Africa and we want to help." Indicating her strong faith, she ended her letter, dated 19 March, 1957: "However, we will leave it for now. If the Good God wants us there, He will provide the means."[6]

During the following months, she gave the matter serious thought and one wonders if she had, in fact, studied and taken to heart the Pope's words in *Fidei Donum*:

> The present situation in Africa, both social and political, requires that a carefully trained Catholic elite be formed at once… How urgent it is then to increase the number of

missionaries able to give a more adequate training to these native leaders.[7]

The proposed site for the school at Abercorn had a special attraction for Mother Antonia. This was the place where she had first set foot on Rhodesian soil in 1954. Despite the hesitancy in her reply to the Bishop's request, she had already started to make remote preparations for the school. Teaching Sisters at home were asked to volunteer for the African Mission. Some of those who volunteered were sent on courses so that they could meet the criteria set out by the Federal Government.

In common with many other missionary endeavours, this school project suffered severe delays and setbacks. The hardest blow came at the end of 1957, when Bishop Van den Biesen was struck down with a serious illness which necessitated his resignation. Like many other missionaries, his intense apostolic activities took their toll on his health. Though still in his prime, he could no longer sustain the huge demands of being a Bishop in this poor, undeveloped part of Central Africa. His place was taken by Father Adolf Furstenberg W.F.[8] who was appointed temporarily in charge of the Vicariate's administration. Under his wise direction and expertise, the soil prepared by his predecessor was to yield an abundant harvest in years to come.

With the entrance of the Sisters of the Sacred Hearts of Jesus and Mary into the education system in Northern Rhodesia, a new era in the history of the Congregation was beginning. In line with the Holy Father's Encyclical and with the Gospel teaching, Mother Antonia's sense of mission enabled her to recognise a pressing need and she did not hesitate to expand the apostolate of the Congregation in Africa.

Chapter 6 – Historic Events

NOTES

1-4. Pope Pius XII. *Encyclical, Fidei Donum.* Rome: Easter Sunday, 21 April, 1957.
5. Van den Biesen, Bishop Joseph. *Letter to Mother Antonia, Zambia*: 6 Feb., 1957.
6. R.M.A. *Letter to Bishop Van den Biesen,* Chigwell: 19 Mar., 1957.
7. *Encyclical,* op. cit. para. 26.
8. Furstenberg, Bishop Adolphe. M.Afr. Born in Iserlohn, Germany, 19 Nov., 1908. Bishop of Abercorn, 1959. Retired 1987. Died in Iserlohn, 12 Nov., 1988.

CHAPTER 7

A Greater Sacrifice

FR. FURSTENBERG was an experienced missionary, having left his native Germany in the 1930s. He had worked tirelessly among the Bemba people in Northern Rhodesia and was familiar with their language and traditions. No sooner had he been appointed Apostolic Administrator than he quickly set to work to continue the previous Bishop's pastoral role, especially in the areas of healthcare and education. Northern Rhodesia was an emerging nation and it was imperative that the Church should endeavour to meet the needs of the people as speedily as possible.

In his first letter to Mother Antonia, 4 April, 1958, he wrote positively about all that had been achieved at Chilonga. He was happy to inform her that an assurance of a grant towards the nurses' training school had been given by the Government Development Commission. His 'one big worry', however, was the electrical and X-ray installations. He wrote:

> But I must first wait for the outcomes of several appeals for financial help before we can undertake this work, which is estimated to cost about £6000. Except for X-ray equipment, this project is not subject to grants from Government.[1]

Progress in the building programme was further delayed by what he referred to as the economic crisis in copper, the country's main source of revenue at that time.

On the same day, he wrote a separate letter to Mother Antonia informing her that he might have to stay in charge of the Vicariate "for a considerable time", and he felt it necessary to keep her informed regarding long-term plans and proposals. He reminded her that Bishop Van den Biesen's plans for the secondary school at Abercorn still stood "and very much so".[2] He also asked her to provide Sisters for schools at Serenji, Chilonga and Mamwe. The Federal Government, he said, was looking to Religious Orders to take responsibility for the state-run hospital at Abercorn. One can only imagine Mother Antonia's reaction to so many requests all at once, but we have her quick response to Father Furstenberg in a letter written on 17 May, 1958:

> We have thought over your Reverence's proposals for your Vicariate and all agree that we would like to help in Northern Rhodesia. Abercorn is where we first set foot in N.R., and we would like our Sisters to be there to undertake the government hospital, for a start with three Sisters. They would be trained nurses, S.R.N, and S.C.M. I should imagine that they would be ready in nine months.[3]

This reply must have been music to Father Furstenberg's ears. It meant that he "could now go ahead with the formal application on behalf of the Sisters to take over Abercorn Government Hospital."[4] This would not involve any expense on the part of the mission or the Congregation. The Nursing Sisters would be paid government salaries, including paid annual leave. Their duties would include the care of African patients as well as the care of a separate block for Europeans who were quite numerous in Abercorn at that time. Doctors and other health care staff were recruited by the Government and were not a concern for Mother Antonia or the Vicariate.

Meanwhile, Fr. Furstenberg focused on Chilonga and on the completion of necessary buildings. A doctor's house had been built and despite recruitment efforts in Europe and North America for a general practitioner, the post had remained vacant for almost three years. In a letter to Canon Bastible, Catholic Missionary Society, Cork, Father Furstenberg wrote:

> We urgently need a doctor, we have tried many times but without success, we would be most grateful if you would help us with this request.[5]

Again, the response was negative. In March, 1959, Mother Antonia kept her promise to send two more Sisters, Sister John Baptist Kennedy and Sister Josephine Guiry, to take up employment at Chilonga Hospital. Father Furstenberg personally supported the Community at Chilonga, encouraging them to rest when necessary, and frequently writing to Mother Antonia to praise their work for the African people. Of his own situation, he wrote:

> We have no news yet about the nomination of a new Bishop. Usually it takes rather a long time. One to two years seems to be the rule.[6]

However, events moved quickly and within six months of his comment Father Furstenberg himself was consecrated Bishop on 29 June, 1959. The Vicariate became the Diocese of Abercorn and he was its first Bishop. From his native town in Iserlohn, Germany, he wrote to Mother Antonia, 4 September, 1959, thanking her for providing Sisters and financial support:

Chapter 7 – A Greater Sacifice

BISHOP ADOLPH FURSTENBERG
Bishop of Mbala 1959 – 1987

> Since my consecration 1 am constantly on the move, giving conferences and sermons all over Germany in order to collect funds for our projects in Abercorn. But I doubt if I can go on as planned. Lately my heart makes funny and unaccustomed jumps... Next week I shall see my doctor in Frankfurt. I will fly back to Africa on 8 December.[7]

Bishop Furstenberg became renowned for fundraising for his Diocese, not only in Germany but also in other European countries.

The proposed secondary school preoccupied Mother Antonia. She continued to ask questions as to when the building would be ready, in fact, for "as many details as possible".[8] Under the direction of Father Boenders M. Afr. the Diocesan Education Secretary, preparations for the school seemed to grow apace. Towards the end of 1959, he sent her the school plans, inviting her comments and informing her of staffing requirements:

> For 2 classes (1961 and 1962), the Principal and Assistant.
> For 4 classes (1963 and 1964), two extra teachers.[9]

On the Bishop's recommendation, Mother Antonia promised to send a Sister for the post of Principal (a graduate) a year earlier so that she could adjust to the country's education system, such as it was in those days. Although knowledge of the Bemba language would be an advantage, it was not essential, since students in the secondary school were taught in the English language. Many of the prospective pupils received their primary education at mission schools where they were well taught and ready for education at secondary level. On hearing from Father Boenders that the Government had changed the site for the new school from Abercorn to Mpika (near Chilonga), Mother Antonia expressed her disappointment:

I have great regard for Abercorn and would like the school to have been there, but I suppose it could not have been changed.[10]

Bishop Furstenberg forged ahead, negotiating with the government and ministers in the Northern Province for permission to buy a piece of land suitable for the site of the new school. After many difficulties, he obtained approval for the purchase of 150 acres on which a White Fathers' mission house, a school and staff houses could be built, with adequate provision for sports' grounds and fruit/vegetable gardens. Writing to Mother Antonia, 21 July, 1960, the Bishop told her:

> You cannot imagine what difficulties we had in order to have the opening of the Girls' Secondary School approved by the government, which is now fixed for August 1961.[11]

The Bishop does not explain the 'difficulties' but these were most likely to have come from the opposition of other faiths or from Government Ministers themselves. It was still a colonial government and the setting up of the first secondary school for African girls in the Northern Province by Catholic missionaries would not be entirely welcome. To be eligible for government grants, the Catholic authorities had to adhere to strict criteria. Prospective pupils would come from a variety of faiths and backgrounds and from distant parts of the territory of Northern Rhodesia.

On receiving a letter from Mother Antonia, dated 14 June, 1960, the Bishop seems to have experienced something of a shock. The teaching Sisters promised for August, 1961 would not arrive until a year later, August 1962. We can understand his dilemma since he had already made a commitment to the Government. In what looks like a passionate plea to Mother

Antonia, he puts before her the serious consequences if she cannot send the Sisters as soon as possible:

> If, however, we would not be able to open in 1962, this would be disastrous... Eight dioceses are counting on our secondary school... it would mean a catastrophe for the Catholic Church in these parts if we did not succeed in establishing the school. Our Catholic girls would be forced to attend Protestant schools, the only alternative... I would beg you rather to undergo heavy sacrifices in the home country than to postpone again the opening of the secondary school here... I have not the least doubt that you do a far greater service to the Church by helping to establish girls' education in this country than by working in Great Britain or elsewhere in Europe. A clear illustration of this is the recent happenings in the Congo. Now that it is too late, everybody agrees that the gravest mistake of the past was the failure to train African leaders of both sexes. Rhodesia is still a haven of peace in the midst of this turmoil.[12]

Mother Antonia's reply to this letter was empathetic and reassuring, and she promised:

> If all works out as we are planning, we should be able to help you. I hope, too, to keep my promise re a donation towards the cost.[13]

She encourages the Bishop to find a site for the school not too near Chilonga. This would give the Sisters a change of house. I know it will mean an extra Superior but I think in the end it would work out better.[14] Within months of the temporary setback, the Bishop happily wrote again, 12 December, 1960, giving a vivid description of the new school's location:

> The site is really beautiful, at the foot of a range of hills (the Muchinga Escarpment) in the proximity of a good peren-

nial stream (the Lwitikila). Half a mile upwards, the stream comes out of a gorge forming several waterfalls. Here, a hydro-electric scheme is planned by the provincial administration. Though near (14 miles) the District Administration – the Boma – it is conveniently secluded as no villages will be allowed to settle between the hills and our side of the stream. Also upstream there are no settlements so that unpolluted water is guaranteed. We could not ask for better conditions.[15]

The Bishop added that he had signed a contract for the school's construction with Keegan-Smith, Lusaka. The building would be 25 miles from Chilonga Hospital so the Sisters could exchange regular visits, which, in the words of the Bishop, would help "to diminish the isolation of the Sisters at Chilonga, which, in my opinion, is their greatest difficulty "[16]

True to his flair for practicality, he outlined for Mother Antonia the estimated cost, £13,100.00, of the first phase of the convent building at the school, which, he remarked,

is rather high in relation to the relatively small initial community. The complete convent will cost about £21,700.00. But the second phase will not be necessary until 1967. If you are in a position to help us financially, this would mean a great diminution of our worries.[17]

In her prompt reply, Mother Antonia promised to send £5,000.00 to the Bishop's account in the Standard Bank of South Africa, Ndola, Northern Rhodesia, adding: "This will help towards your heavy outlay."[18]

For the Bishop and Mother Antonia, the setting up of a secondary school in a developing country was an entirely new venture. In doing so, they both shared the common vision of bringing the light of the Gospel into the lives of young women by providing them with education, which is their inalienable right. One cannot but notice the sense of urgency which is reflected in their correspondence at this stage, and this is even more evident in the letters of the General Secretary for Catholic Education, Father Colm O'Riordan, SJ. Writing to Mother Antonia from Lusaka, 22 January, 1961, he pointed out that the first class in the school was due to begin in August of that year. He strongly recommended that the new Principal should come to Rhodesia three months in advance so that she could become familiar with the local problems and the educational set-up. He advised:

> It would assist her very much if she could arrange to stay for some time with the Franciscan Sisters (O.S.F.), Maramba, Livingstone, Northern Rhodesia, who are running the only Catholic School for African girls in the territory at present. They will be in the best position to advise you about any problems or queries you may have... I appreciate very much your sacrifices for the cause of girls' education in Northern Rhodesia.[19]

At the Mother House in Chigwell, the two Sisters chosen to start the first phase of the school were already appointed. They were: Sister John Eudes (Teresa Mulroy), a trained graduate from Cork University, and Sister Agnes (Eileen Hennebry), a trained teacher from Notre Dame College, Liverpool, who also held a diploma from the National College for Domestic Subjects, London. Both Sisters were well qualified to satisfy the requirements of the Federal Government's Ministry of Education, and they eagerly awaited the challenge of venturing into the unknown.

Chapter 7 – A Greater Sacifice

The next few years were to present many problems and difficulties for the Sisters of the Sacred Hearts of Jesus and Mary in Africa, but they rose to the challenge, and the Congregation could now add the words "Nursing and Teaching Missionaries" to the description of their apostolate.

NOTES
1. Furstenberg, Fr. A. *Letter to R.M.A.* (1), Zambia: 4 April, 1958.
2. ibid. *Letter to R.M.A.* (2), Zambia: 4 April, 1958
3. R.M.A. *Letter to Fr. Furstenberg,* Chigwell: 17 May, 1958.
4. Furstenberg, Fr. A. *Letter to R.M.A.* (3), Zambia: 1958.
5. ibid. *Letter to Canon Bastibte,* Catholic Missionary Society, Cork, Ireland.
6. Furstenberg, Bishop A. *Letter to R.M.A.* Zambia: Jan. 1959.
7. ibid. *Letter to R.M.A.* Germany: 4 Sept. 1959.
8. Boenders, Fr. M. M.Afr. *Letter to Mother Antonia,* Zambia: 1959.
9. R.M.A. *Letter to Fr. M. Boenders.* M. Afr., Chigwell: 1959.
10. Furstenberg, Bishop A. *Letter to R.M.A.* Zambia: 21 July, 1960.
11. ibid. *Letter to R.M.A.* Zambia: Aug. 1961.
13, 14. R.M.A. *Letter to Bishop Furstenberg.* Chigwell: 14 June, 1960.
15-17. Furstenberg, Bishop A. *Letter to R.M.A.* Zambia: 12 Dec. 1960.
18. R.M.A. *Letter to Bishop Fustenberg.* Chigwell: 1961.
19. O'Riordan, Fr. Colm S.J. General Secretary. Catholic Education. *Letter to R.M.A.* Zambia: 22 Jan. 1961.

CHAPTER 8

The Winds of Change

THE PROPHETIC WORDS spoken by Harold Macmillan, British Prime Minister, to the South African Parliament in 1960 – "The wind of change is blowing through this continent"[1] – were slowly becoming a reality, as the 1960s ushered in phenomenal change, not only in Africa but throughout the world. Pope John XXIII, who had been Pope for just 90 days, announced unexpectedly on 25 January, 1959 his plan to promote the Church's twenty-first Ecumenical Council. This finally opened on 12 October, 1962 and concluded on 8 December 1965. The pastoral tone set by Pope John in his opening address to the Council Fathers, just nine months before his death in June, 1963, was to dominate the Council's deliberations. The great documents arising from these deliberations, especially the Constitution on the Church, are especially noteworthy because of the concern they expressed for the poor, for their insistence on the unity of the human family and for their emphasis on the Christian's duty to help build a just and peaceful world. This great Ecumenical Council has been seen as an extraordinary movement of the Holy Spirit across the world.

Other remarkable events were also unfolding in the early sixties. The election of the first Catholic President of the United

Chapter 8 – The Winds of Change

States, John F. Kennedy, took place in November, 1960. Within the brief period of his presidency, (he was assassinated on 22 November, 1963) he fought fearlessly for basic human rights, for the equality of all people and against racial discrimination. He appealed not only to his 'fellow Americans' but also to the whole world. Conscious of the need for change, he reminded his listeners that *"Change is the law of life and those who look only to the past or present are certain to miss the future."*[2]

As we have seen already, Mother Antonia was not fearful of embracing change when it meant extending the Congregation's mission in the Church and in the world. She was acutely aware that the establishment of further foundations in Northern Rhodesia would involve an uphill struggle both in human resources and financial terms. She felt urged on by the conviction that future generations of the African people, especially women and children, would be denied a basic quality of life if members of religious orders like ourselves were not prepared to make bigger sacrifices. She wished to see the Sisters of her own Congregation play their part alongside other Religious Orders from Canada, France, U.S.A., Germany, Belgium and Ireland, in the fields of healthcare and education. The early sixties saw a large influx of young missionaries into Northern Rhodesia, enthusiastically assisting the people along the path to full independence in 1964, under the new name of Zambia.

These were exciting times not only for the Zambian people but also for expatriates who were happy to face a variety of challenges. Mother Antonia's dream school at Lwitikila was gradually taking shape. She had promised to send two Sisters in August, 1961, to set up the one-form entry school planned by Bishop Furstenberg. Sister John Eudes Mulroy and Sister Eileen

Hennebry arrived by air in Ndola, via Entebbe, Uganda, on 10 August. As recommended by the National Education Secretary, Fr. Colm O'Riordan S.J., their orientation period was spent with the Franciscan Sisters at Maramba, Livingstone. There, Sister Mary Carmel explained the curriculum and timetable for the African Girls' School, not too different from that of a grammar school in Britain with the exception of very different extra-curricular activities. The visit to Livingstone gave the Sisters the opportunity to see the beauty of this part of Central Africa, including the spectacular Victoria Falls on the mighty Zambezi River. The journey by road also took them along a route through the country's more developed southern province south of Lusaka.

The first disappointment awaiting the Sisters on their arrival at Chilonga was the news that the school building at Lwitikila would not be ready for several months. Classrooms and two dormitories to accommodate them were prepared at the White Sisters' mission at Ilondola, 160 miles away. Much more alarming was the other news that Bishop Furstenberg had forbidden them to travel any further because of serious political disturbances. These were created by the followers of Alice Lenshina, the foundress of a Protestant breakaway Church in the Northern Province. The aim of this group was to spread political and religious propaganda for future independence.[3]

Describing the havoc wreaked by the Lenshina riots, Sister John Eudes wrote in her diary, 7 October, 1961:

> Over forty schools were burnt down, roads were blocked with trees and Europeans were attacked on the way... On Thursday, the last day of August, the Fathers brought word that we could travel from Mpika Police Station with a convoy the following morning. At Mpika, we picked up

our police escort and set out for Ilondola which is in the heart of the bush. Already, thirty pupils had arrived at the mission, much to the amazement of the White Fathers, who did not expect them to have found their way along the hazardous routes affected by the Lenshina riots.[4]

Delays and disappointments did not dampen the spirit of enthusiasm reflected in the opening of the new school on 12 September. Representatives of the Federal Government, The Ministry of Education, the Provincial Education Office and the Diocese of Abercorn were in attendance. Sisters Kieran Marie and Josephine provided the buffet lunch, taken all the 160 miles from Chilonga in as many cool bags as they could find. The Diocesan Education Secretary, Fr. Reuter W.F., welcomed everyone, especially Sisters John Eudes and Eileen, and wished them success in their daunting mission. The students were all boarders and two dormitories were provided by the White Sisters. Their uniform was a pink dress with a white collar and a white beret. Since the opening of the school was delayed by six weeks, there was no time to waste and classes began immediately.

The school syllabus was quite demanding and students were expected to be ready to take the Cambridge Overseas G.C.S.E. Examination at the end of four years, with a public examination at the end of Form 2. To begin with, the subjects taken were English Language and Literature, History, Geography, Maths, Religion, Latin and Home Economics, which included Cookery and Needlework. The latter subject was compulsory and considered an essential part of the young girls' education. The two Sisters were extremely busy both in the classroom and with the supervision of study in the evenings. Lessons were taught between 7.00 am. and 1.30 pm. with a half-hour break at 10.30 am. as this was the coolest part of the day and also took in the hours of daylight. Before classes began, students were expected to leave their dormitories spick and span. Extra-curricular activities took place in the late afternoon and were mostly connected with gardening, digging, sowing seeds, planting, irrigating. These outdoor activities were done in small groups in a recreational manner, with girls singing happily in their traditional Bemba way. Most of the students were accustomed to this work in the rural environment from which they came. This period also provided the Sisters with the opportunity to become acquainted with them in an informal way, and to learn expressions and customs of the Bemba tribe.

The Home Economics room, in Sr. Eileen's charge, proved very popular for cooking, baking and catering, and the girls took readily to learning the skills required for budgeting and dietary planning. Many students had a natural flair for sewing, and teaching them to design and make simple garments on a sewing machine was a pleasure. Besides teaching other subjects, Sr. Eileen also gave singing lessons in English. It was not long before English songs and hymns were adapted by the girls to the harmonious sounds and rhythms of the Bemba choral tradition.[5]

At the end of the first two weeks, Bishop Furstenberg paid a visit to the new school. He told the Sisters that he was amazed at the progress made in such a short time. Sister John Eudes wrote:

> He gave us much credit for our efforts. He said he was determined that the new school will be built and open by July, 1962. He gave us great confidence.[6]

From this simple beginning at Ilondola in Northern Rhodesia, the Sisters of the Sacred Hearts of Jesus and Mary began their ministry of educating African girls. Under the direction of Sr. John Eudes, the school soon became a centre of excellence. Adapting to a different culture, and, at the same time, educating young women for the future of the newly independent country, was indeed a constant challenge in the years ahead. The results proved that this challenge had been successfully met. Mother Antonia's dream was fast becoming a reality.

NOTES
1. Macmillan, Rt. Hon. Harold. *Speech to the Parliament of South Africa*, Pretoria: 3 Feb., 1960.
2. Kennedy, President J. F. *Address to the German Assembly at Paolkirche: Frankfurt*, 25 June, 1963.
3. Hinfelaar, H.F. *History of the Catholic Church in Zambia: 1895-1995*. Lusaka, Bookworld Publishers: 2004. p. 185
4. Mulroy, Sr. John Eudes. *Diary*, Illondola: 7 Oct. 1961.
5. Hennebry, Sr. Eileen. *Interviewed by Sr. Austin*, Chigwell: Aug. 2012.
6. Mulroy, Sr. John Eudes. op.cit. 10 Oct., 1961.

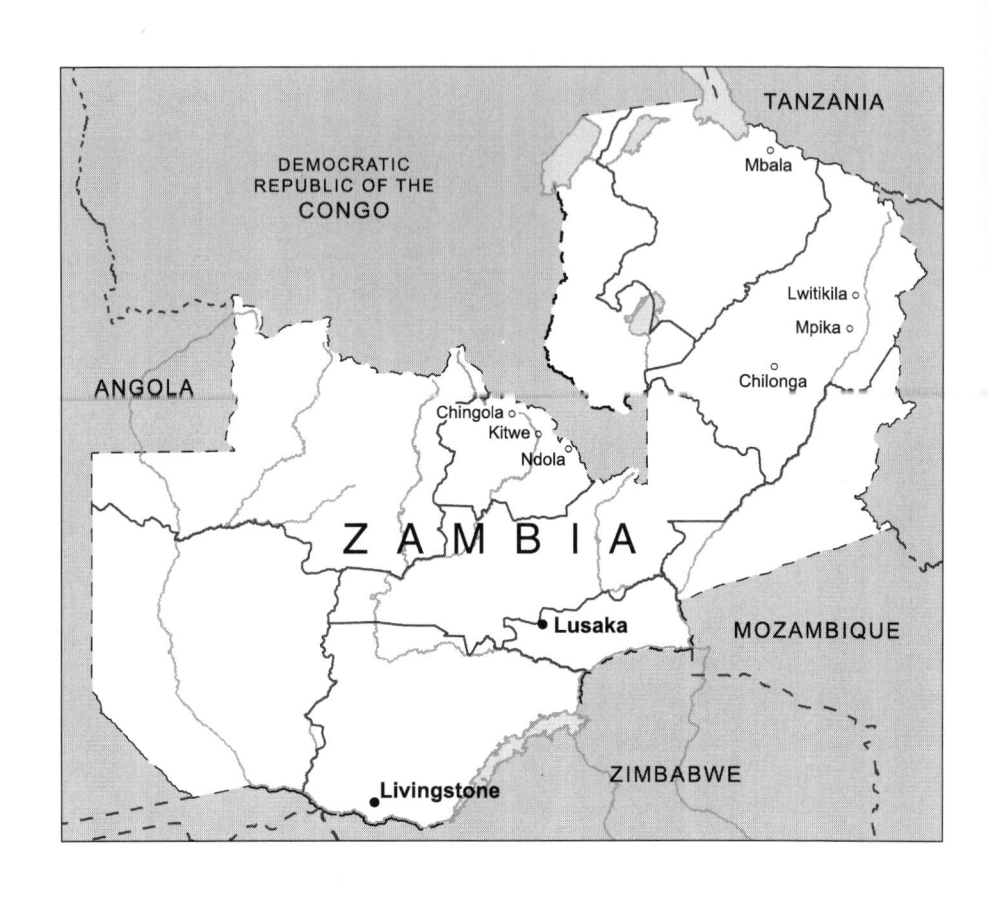

Map of Zambia

Missions of the Sisters of the Sacred Hearts of Jesus and Mary
1956 – 2006

Chapter 9

Eventful Years

Looking Forward with Hope

WHILST THE FIRST PHASE of the Lwitikila school (known then as the Sacred Heart Secondary School) was moving forward, the mission at Chilonga was expanding. The arrival of a resident doctor from America on 6 August, 1960 meant that the Sisters could proceed with the building of the Nurses' Training School. Its architect was Brother Koch W.F. and the building contractor was Keegan-Smith, Lusaka.[1] Approval was granted by the Director of Medical Services, and the Provincial Medical Officer, Dr. Braithwaite, awarded a grant to the mission of £778.13.7. This addition to the existing mission hospital was described by Mother Antonia as "excellent in every detail".[2] Sr. Josephine Guiry was the first Sister Tutor and she began classes with eight young African women on 1 September, 1962.

From 16 May until 10 June, 1962, Mother Antonia visited Northern Rhodesia for the second time. She was accompanied by Mother Bernadette, Secretary General, later Mother General. This time the flight was from Gatwick, with stops at Entebbe and Ndola. In her letter of 12 June, she described the purpose of her visit:

> The most important purpose of our visit, after the visitation of the Sisters, was the consideration of the Government (Colonial) offer of the African hospital which the Director of Medical Services wished us to take over. I can assure you it is no picnic. It comprises the African hospital at Abercorn, 240 miles from Chilonga, with 90 beds; small European hospital, 8 dispensaries and a leper colony some distance away. I hesitated at the undertaking, but the Sisters assured me that they were willing to tackle it and work will commence there in October. A house (for the Sisters) is available at the moment but we propose to build a convent later with God's help.[3]

During her meeting with Dr. Webster, Director of Medical Services in Lusaka, Mother Antonia formally signed the contract agreeing that she would staff the Government hospital with four qualified nurses. Once this business was completed, the two visitors, accompanied by Sisters Kieran Marie and John Baptist, made their journey of nearly 400 miles to Chilonga along the Great North Road. Seven years had passed since Mother Antonia, now 73 years old, had travelled this same route. Three hundred miles of the road still remained potholed and rough as they revisited Mkushi, Serenji and finally Chilonga, where they were warmly welcomed by the Fathers, Sisters, staff and children. Mother Antonia wrote in her diary:

> What surprised us was the unexpected pleasantness of the surroundings and the great work done by the Sisters. We were very tired after the long journey over the rough roads.[4]

On her return to Chilonga she met Bishop Furstenberg, who once again discussed with her the needs of the proposed mission at Abercorn. Characteristically thinking ahead, he asked her if she could also consider staffing the T.B. Unit, 15 miles from Abercorn, and if she could possibly send a Sister to help the women on the mission "in the running of their little homes."[5]

What had been achieved at Chilonga was an edifying experience for Mothers Antonia and Bernadette. Since the arrival of Dr. Wehler, the number of outpatients at the hospital had exceeded 2,200 in the years 1960-61. With the installation of X-ray equipment, bought with a donation of £1,760.00 from the people of Germany, the hospital was highly regarded for its efficiency and professionalism. Mother Antonia had high praise for the Doctor, his wife Doris and their 'wonderful family'[6] of nine children, six of whom were at boarding school in Ndola. Dr. Wehler was a graduate of Jefferson Medical College, Philadelphia, and was licensed to practice surgery in the States of Pennsylvania and Montana. He was totally committed to the service of the sick in Africa. At Chilonga, the two visitors also encountered a number of volunteers from Holland and Germany, to whom Mother Antonia referred as

> boys and girls who came out to help on the missions – plumbers, electricians, carpenters, brick makers and brick layers, nurses and path. lab. technicians. A wonderful apostolate![7]

These voluntary helpers were supported by the newly-formed aid organization Misereor in Germany. All of them were highly skilled and greatly appreciated by missionaries, especially in the initial stage of setting up a mission.

It was Ascension Day, Thursday, 30 May, 1962, when the two visitors eventually arrived in Abercorn, the goal of their journey. They were welcomed at the White Fathers' Mission by Fathers Boenders and Levesque, Brother Koch and the 'German and Dutch boys'.[8] After meeting with the District Commissioner at the Boma (government offices), they were taken on a tour of the government hospital

> where the Matron and doctor showed us everything – a very, very poor show indeed. There were patients all over the place, inside and outside, and we gained a very bad impression.[9]

Fr. Boenders then took the Sisters to see the house in Little Poland Road, which would be the temporary home of the Sisters before they took up their duties in the hospital. A major concern was the slow progress of the building at Lwitikila (named Chikwanda after the local village). She observed: "The convent will be lovely with twelve rooms and a chapel".[10] She questioned if the school building would be ready by 1 August, just two months away.

On her return to Chilonga, Mother Antonia did not hide her dismay when describing the impoverished conditions at Lwitikila School, and wondered if the Sisters could possibly work in such dire conditions. But, as already pointed out, they were ready to meet the challenge. She informed the Community of her anxiety: "How can I send my Sisters to such a place? It's nowhere ready."[11] She thought the location was rather isolated, a long way from the main road with an unfinished driveway, but she added:

> It is considered a very good site for various reasons, near Chilonga Hospital, the Boma, where the District Commissioner and Police reside, and water supply.[12]

At Ilondola, Sisters John Eudes and Eileen were preparing for the summer vacation. The next step was the transfer of the

Chapter 9 – Eventful Years

school by the beginning of August to the new site at Lwitikila, where it would be enlarged to a two-form entry, bringing the total entry to ninety students. Transferring the classes from an established mission to one where facilities were incomplete must have been a daunting task. From the follow-up to the Visitation of Northern Rhodesia we can assume that Mother Antonia was fully aware of this. On her return to the Mother House at Chigwell, she consulted with two Sisters who she believed were capable setting the mission school on a firm foundation. They were Sister Imelda (Monica McMahon) and Sister Euphemia (Mary A. Collins). Both were experienced Sisters with the faith and commitment necessary for this pioneering task.

In the language of today, Sisters Imelda and Euphemia were excellent crisis managers. However, the problems confronting them at Lwitikila surpassed their worst expectations. By the end of July, the roofing was not finished and the Sisters recall "sleeping under the stars."[13] In order to have the school ready for the scheduled opening on 1 August, they had to scramble to organise classrooms, furniture, dormitories and dining/cooking facilities. Fr. Kohle, a German White Father with over forty years experience in Africa, was appointed chaplain to the school. He proved himself an asset to the Sisters, who were complete strangers here. The Sisters in Chilonga helped with the setting up of the kitchen and providing food. Sr. Imelda, now aged 64 and who had volunteered to go to Africa, had a gift for forming community and was a natural home-maker. It did not take her long to get the wood-burning cooker working and to produce tasty meals. Her sense of humour was invaluable, especially when times were tough. With no lighting in the mission, except candles and one tilly lamp, and no electricity, there were several mishaps, especially when there was no twilight and darkness came suddenly at 6.00 pm.

Sr. Euphemia had not volunteered for the African mission, yet she accepted Mother Antonia's request to become the first School Principal at Lwitikila. At the age of 43 she was well-experienced in the fields of education and administration. As a trained graduate of London University, she had a quick grasp of facts and was a good organiser. With Sisters John Eudes and Eileen, she had the school ready on time. Under the Federal Government, mission schools were part-funded and were therefore subject to regular inspections. From the very beginning, Lwitikila met the high expectations of the Inspectors from the Ministry of Education, who did not always take kindly to schools and colleges under the direction of Catholic missionaries. Despite the numerous hitches and setbacks, the school soon became renowned for high academic achievement. Students were keen to learn and to strive towards the high standards set for them. This was the beginning of a centre of learning with a bright and exciting future.

Whilst Lwitikila was being set up, Mother Antonia was busy preparing for the new foundation at Abercorn. On 15 August, 1962, Sister Amabilis (Sarah Hennessy) and her sister, Sister Romana (Rita Hennessy) left Chigwell to join Sisters Kieran Marie and La Salette at Chilonga. All four of them were assigned to the Government Hospital. They were registered nurses and midwives and were given salaries and conditions similar to other Government health employees. Sister Kieran Marie was appointed matron and she was also chosen to lead the community in this new foundation. With six years experience in Northern Rhodesia, she and Sister la Salette were no strangers to the difficulties and privations involved in this new mission.

Staff already working in the hospital resented the coming of the Sisters and it took strongly-worded correspondence from Bishop Furstenberg to affirm their commitment and professionalism. The new mission at Abercorn was dear to Mother Antonia's heart. It was, in her own words, "the first place we set foot on Northern Rhodesian soil."[14]

Situated on the southern tip of Lake Tanganika, Abercorn in those days was an important centre for scientific and agricultural research and for industries connected with fisheries on the lake. It had its own airport serving the Red Locusts Scientists, veterinary services, flying doctors, and it had a direct link with the Copperbelt and Lusaka. It did not have the same sense of isolation as Chilonga and Lwitikila. The four Sisters, whose work was mainly at the African Hospital, had an outreach to dispensaries, the European Hospital and the leper colony, and they quickly formed good relationships with all those involved. They had come to Abercorn two years before the country had attained independence (October, 1964) and they had witnessed some of the political unrest leading up to that event. Today, after 50 years, some of the local people can still recall the kindness and compassion shown to them by the Sisters. One testimonial comes from Mr. Mpunu Mutambo, who, as a member of the Freedom Fighters, was incarcerated in Abercorn prison under the last colonial District Commissioner, Mr. Simon, who was also the Police Chief and Magistrate for the area. For his alleged crime, the order was given for Mr. Mutambo to be beaten, and as a result he was admitted to hospital. Here he was treated by Sister La Salette "with great kindness" and Doctor Taylor demanded that he was not to "receive any more strokes".[15] Among Mr. Mutambo's other memories was the lady, Doctor Trant, renowned for her service to the African people, especially women and children. She worked in close collaboration with the Sisters in the early days.

The foundation made at Abercorn (name changed to Mbala in 1964) was the starting point of a long and varied ministry to the people of this region. Perhaps Mother Antonia foresaw this when she wrote to the Congregation after her last visit in June, 1962:

> I must say how impressed I was at the tremendous amount of hard work that has been done in Africa since our brave pioneers went out in 1956, and earnestly hope that the Chigwell spirit which these dear Sisters have established in the heart of Africa will ever be maintained by those who follow.[16]

This chapter about the eventful 1960s would be incomplete without recording the special contribution made by the young men and women volunteers from Misereor, the German organisation already referred to. Among these was Mr. Gerhard Merschmeyer who set up a brick factory at Lwitikila to supply bricks for all the mission buildings during this period of expansion. Using the machine donated by his organisation, he produced three million bricks between April, 1964 and May, 1966. In addition to giving employment to local men, he trained them in skills, using the local clay, enabling them to produce bricks to form strong building materials for their own homes.

Like many young people venturing into unfamiliar territory without an adequate orientation programme, Gerhard's experiences were somewhat unique. One such experience was when he stunned a snake and carried it aloft as he rode round the school campus while the young girls screamed their heads off! Without realising that catching a snake like this was taboo in the Bemba culture, he returned to the factory to find his workmen

Chapter 9 – Eventful Years

in total silence, refusing to speak to him for not respecting their culture. Here, Gerhard himself takes up the story:

> That evening Bishop Furstenberg ordered me to leave the place and come to Abercorn until he could explain what happened to the local Chief, Chikwanda. To redeem my reputation among my workmen I had to perform some action that proved I was not just a clever man but also a very brave one. How could I do this? It was a stroke of luck that the Bishop asked me to drive Michael Keegan back to Lwitikila, a distance of two hundred and fifty miles late that night. At about 4.00 am the following morning as we approached the Chilonga/Mpika turn, I saw two tiny spotlights before me. As I passed the place at high speed the front bumper of the car was hit by something, I could not tell what it was. Michael Keegan forced me to stop and told me to go into reverse gear to find out the cause. As we drove back we both saw an animal lying on the road. Coming closer we saw a leopard!!! Never in my life did I feel such relief in my stomach as I knew my reputation had been restored at that moment. We took the bag home as Michael wanted the skin as it was without any bullet hole. The following morning I drove the car with the dead leopard in it down to the brickyard. I told the story to the curious workers who embraced me. They were so happy to have me back and all was forgiven. That day we produced 15,000 bricks, a record never to be repeated![17]

This is just a sample of the wonderful work done by volunteers. Their help was invaluable and they contributed in no small way to the development of our missions in Zambia.

The 1960s were indeed eventful years! The Congregation of the Sacred Hearts of Jesus and Mary could now be numbered among the many Missionary Congregations of the Church.

NOTES
1. Keegan, Michael, Construction Engineer. Born in Galway, Ireland.
2, 3. R.M.A. *Circular Letter to the Congregation*, Chigwell: June, 1961.
4, 5. R.M.A. *Diary*, Zambia: 1961.
6. *Medical Records*, Lusaka Archives, Zambia: 1962.
7-12. R.M.A. op. cit.
13. Hennebry, Sr. Eileen, *Account of Early Days*, Zambia: 1962.
14. R.M.A. op. cit.
15. Mutambo, Mr. Mbala. *Interview with Sr. Austin Gallagher*, Zambia: 25 May, 2010.
16. R.M.A. op. cit.
17. Merschmeyer, Gerhard. *Memories of Zambia in the 1960s*, Germany: Dec. 2012.

CHAPTER 10

On the Edge of a New Era

THE DECREES of the Second Vatican Council (1962-1965) exerted worldwide influence and nowhere more than in mission territory. Convoking the Council, 29 December, 1961, Pope John XXIII spoke of humanity being on the edge of a new era when tasks of immense gravity and amplitude await the Church.

> It is a question in fact of bringing the modern world into contact with the vivifying and perennial energies of the Gospel.[1]

Whilst these words were relevant to any part of the world, they had special significance for developing countries, where even today education and health care remain matters of urgency.

The hospital ministries begun by the Sisters of the Sacred Hearts of Jesus and Mary at Chilonga (1956) and Abercorn (1962) made steady progress throughout the 1960s. The intake of the new Nurses' Training School increased and earned a good reputation for the calibre of its graduates, who were employed in hospitals throughout the country. The colonial government promised to replace the dilapidated hospital at Abercorn with a new modern structure, but this was not to happen immediately. In the meantime, the Sisters purchased a plot of land for the site of the new convent on which Mother Antonia had proposed to build. This was close to the White Fathers' mission. First it was necessary to have the Congregation registered under the Lands Ordinance of Rhodesia and Nyasaland. On the advice of Bishop Furstenberg,[2] Mother Antonia appointed three Trustees on 19 August. 1963. They were:

> Sr. Imelda (Monica McMahon) Lwitikila
> Sister Kieran Marie (Eileen Pilkington) Abercorn
> Sister John Baptist (Clare Kennedy) Chilonga

The new convent, together with the piece of land, would become the property of the Congregation, with the official title deeds sent to Mother Antonia at Chigwell. The building contractor (Keegan-Smith, Lusaka), built a fine two-storey convent and chapel, following plans and recommendations from Sister Kieran Marie.[3]

The new convent was a welcome change for the Sisters, who were working under difficult conditions at the existing hospital. It also provided accommodation for Sisters visiting from remote missions. Sufficient land remained for beautifully landscaped gardens and plots for fruit trees and vegetables. Today, after fifty years, this convent still provides facilities for a variety of ministries. Sister Kieran Marie had planned wisely, and, without knowing it, Mother Antonia had left a valuable legacy for future generations.

From 1963 onwards, Lwitikila school increased its annual intake from 60 students in August, 1962 to 220 in January, 1966, the year Form 3 commenced. With help from German volunteers, Gerhard (brick maker/layer) and Anton (electrician), eight classrooms were completed by August, 1965. These included two Science Laboratories, a Home Economics Room, an Administration Block and extra dormitories. Mother Antonia continued to staff the school with teaching Sisters-Sister John Vincent (Mary McDonald), July, 1963, Sister Austin (Brigid Gallagher), January, 1964, Sister Angela Pycroft, September, 1964.

The month of September, 1963, was a time of change within the Congregation itself. At the General Chapter, Mother Antonia, who had been Superior General since 1945, was replaced by Mother Bernadette, (Mary Flavin), the Secretary General. She had accompanied Mother Antonia on her last visit to Africa in 1962 and shared with her predecessor a great love for Africa and its people. In collaboration with Father O'Riordan S.J., the Education Secretary in Northern Rhodesia, she recruited lay teachers for the Lwitikila school from the Missionary Association in England.

Independence Day came on 24 October, 1964, when the country of Northern Rhodesia became Zambia, named after one of Africa's greatest rivers, the Zambezi, famed for the Victoria Falls. In the 1950s, the waters of the river had been harnessed to supply electricity to Southern Rhodesia (now Zimbabwe), and to parts of Zambia, as far north as the Copperbelt There was a strong feeling of joyful expectancy throughout the country leading up to independence, as everyone awaited the birth of a new African nation. Even in the most remote places in the bush, people happily chanted: "One Zambia! One Nation!" The students at Lwitikila sang their new national anthem with gusto in Bemba and in English:

"Stand and sing of Zambia proud and free!
Land of work and joy and unity"

Of keen interest, too, was the country's new flag, symbolising the rich resources of the country, its forests, its soil and mineral wealth, with a hovering eagle, a symbol of the spirit of its people to triumph over adversity. On the eve of Independence Day, teachers and students listened to the radio, despite the muffled reception, to hear President Kaunda address the new nation. He urged everyone to work hard to develop their country's resources, describing Zambia as "a Land of Promise".[4]

As the country celebrated in every town and village on 24 October, the Lwitikila Sisters and students made their way precariously in open trucks to the Boma grounds at Mpika, to the accompaniment of flag-waving and joyful singing in the Bemba language. It was a thrilling moment when the new flag was hoisted to the sound of drum beats and excited clapping. Tribal dances were performed by local artists who were enthusiastically applauded. A special treat for the occasion was the meat donated by the local chiefs to the people and students alike. Expatriates present at the Mpika event entered happily into the spirit of the celebration.[5] It was the birthday of a new nation, and in the words of Pope John XXIII, there was the sense of being "on the edge of a new era".[6]

The enthusiasm generated by the Independence celebrations was reflected especially in the field of education. New secondary schools were springing up in every province, staffed mainly by expatriate teachers, Religious and Lay. Many of these were on contract for two to three years. They taught the secondary school curriculum and initiated outdoor pursuits in agriculture, sports and fund-raising. At Lwitikila, Patrick and

Chapter 10 – On the Edge of a New Era

Mary James developed drama to a professional level, even producing Shakespearean plays. With help from the students, Patrick used his building skills to construct an outdoor theatre which was to serve future generations of performers. Michael Davis undertook the daunting task of clearing the bush to make way for a 400 metre sports track. The work force that was tarmacking a local section of the Great North Road at the time assisted with bulldozers and other heavy equipment. The track became a much-used facility for games and sports. In addition to running the Modern Languages Department, Mrs. Catherine Davis set up the Rangers, who cultivated the school garden. They grew a variety of vegetables which they sold to the Crested Crane Hotel in Mpika, thus raising funds for the school. Two young Voluntary Service Overseas teachers, Nuala Breen and Patricia Smith, on contract for one year, played a significant part in the development of the school by organising games and sports.

Sister Euphemia placed great emphasis on academic achievement. It was due to her, in no small measure, that the school was delivering the full curriculum by 1965. The students in Form 2 in 1965 were 75% successful. When this same Form sat the Cambridge Overseas G.C.E. in 1968, there were 89% passes. Considering the school's location in such a remote part of the country, this was a remarkable achievement. Unfortunately, classes were severely disrupted when, on 7 September, 1965, Sister Angela Pycroft, Head of Science, was involved in a car accident on the Great North Road near Chikwanda village. She was initiating Sister Stanislaus, newly arrived from the U.K., into driving on bush roads when their car skidded into a trench. Sister Angela suffered permanent injuries to her back and had to return home. Not only had she been responsible for a successful Science Department, but she had also played a leading role in the school's outdoor pursuits programme, especially in tennis. Her absence was keenly felt. On returning home, she taught Science and Mathematics from a wheelchair, and later became a computer expert.

Within a few years, Lwitikila school was nationally commended for its performance in Mathematics. Sister Mary Costello, who arrived in 1965, and who had recently graduated from Cork University, took the teaching of this subject to such a high level that the school became a member of the Mathematical Association of Zambia.

Students participated in international contests as far away as Kenya, Uganda and Tanzania. The Lwitikila environment provided a paradise for botanists and geographers. A wide variety of flora and fauna and unique physical features were on the doorstep, and students enjoyed regular expeditions without having to travel too far. Fieldwork involved map-reading and ecology.

As Lwitikila was a Christian school, the students took their faith very seriously. Most of them belonged to devout Christian families and had been instructed in the Christian faith by missionary priests and their catechists. Bishop Furstenberg, who attended the sessions of the Vatican Council during the early 60s, brought back reports of matters affecting the life of the Church throughout the world. One major and very welcome change was the celebration of the Mass in the vernacular and female altar servers came as a welcome surprise. A new church, designed by Brother Koch W.F., was formally opened in 1965, and it had all the requirements for liturgical changes. Liturgies were lively as students entered wholeheartedly into religious celebrations, singing harmoniously in their native language. The school was fortunate to have Father Kohle W.F. as its chaplain. With his long experience of 42 years as a missionary, he was familiar with the language and customs of the Bemba people. He had a good rapport with young people and they valued his weekly instruction. One student said of him at the time: "Father knows exactly what we need to know at this stage."[7] Clashes of culture were not uncommon among expatriate teachers and students, sometimes ending in strike action on the part of students. Father Kohle had the amazing gift of being able to negotiate a peaceful outcome.

The year 1965 brought about other changes in the Zambian missions. Sister Imelda had to return to the U.K for health reasons. She had been superior of the convent in Lwitikila since the beginning. She had established a warm, welcoming community and was at pains to continue the spirit of the Congregation. Her leadership not only supported the education ministry but also gave cohesion and stability to the group. Another blow to the newly-founded mission was the sudden death of the Superior General on 25 October, 1965. She had been in office for just over two years. Like her predecessor, she had made big financial sacrifices to support the new apostolates in Africa. Despite the demands of the home missions, she did not hesitate to send Sisters to Zambia when they were needed. Her successor was Mother Etheldreda (Mary Gleeson) who was Superior General until 1979.

Almost one year to the day after Sister Angela's accident, disaster struck again. Sister Euphemia, the School Principal, was killed in a car accident on 13 September, 1966. She was returning from Lusaka with two new teachers when the car, driven by Brother Gunther W.F., ran into a mound of sand. Late that night, the Sisters at Lwitikila received a telegram radioed to Mpika Police Station which said:

> There was an accident on the Great North Road, twenty miles north of Serenje. One fatality believed to be Sister Euphemia.[8]

Father van Dorst, a White Father based at Serenje mission, had identified her. Next day, he and his confrere, Father Corbeil, brought her coffin back to Lwitikila. The Requiem Mass was concelebrated by a large number of White Fathers, the chief celebrant being Father Levesque. Her remains were buried in a clearing in the bush a few hundred yards from the school, amid great sadness expressed by the students, who piled branches of purple bougainvillea on her grave.[9]

The death of Sister Euphemia had a profound effect on the mission. It was obvious from the tributes to her that came flooding in from education officials in Lusaka and Kasama that she was an outstanding educator and administrator. In those days there were no telephones in remote parts of Africa, so it was no surprise that members of her family in Ireland learned of her death from television and radio. The Collins family mourned her passing in her birthplace near Athenry, Co. Galway, in the U.S.A. and in Australia.

The death of the first Principal of Lwitikila Secondary School marked the end of the first phase of its history. Continuity was assured when Sister John Vincent stepped into the role of Principal in October, 1966. It was a hard act to follow, but in the years ahead she continued to develop the school with enthusiasm, zeal and competence.

Chapter 10 – On the Edge of a New Era

NOTES

1. Pope John XXIII. *Address on the Convocation of the Second Vatican Council*; Rome, 29 Dec. 1961.
2. Furstenberg, Bishop Adolf. *Letter to Mother Antonia*, Zambia: 12 Aug., 1963.
3. R.M.A. *Letter to Bishop Furstenberg*, Chigwell: 19 Aug., 1963.
4. Kaunda, Kenneth, President of Zambia. *Address to the Nation*, Zambia: 23 Oct., 1964.
5. Burke, Sr. Ellen. *Memories of Independence Day*, Zambia: 15 Aug., 1964.
6. Pope John XXIII. op. cit.
7-9. Lwitikila Secondary School. *Journal*, Lwitikila: 1966.

CHAPTER 11

'Energy and resourcefulness'
(President Kenneth Kaunda)

TOWARDS THE END of the 1960s, the Sisters of the Sacred Hearts of Jesus and Mary witnessed rapid expansion in their Health Care and Education ministries. At Lwitikila, the school continued to be staffed by Sisters from Chigwell. In 1967, Sister Perpetua (Marcella Clerkin) was appointed Head of the English Department. She was a gifted teacher and her lessons helped to raise standards in that subject. Sister Scholastica (Bridget McCourt) became Head of Home Economics in 1968, and she made a great difference to the life of the school in the areas of Cookery, Needlework, Hygiene, Budgeting and Child Development. Lay teachers, on contract from the U.K. and Ireland, continued to arrive, so there were no lapses in the delivery of the school curriculum and extra-curricular activities.

On 2 November, 1968, after his first visit to the school, President Kaunda wrote to the Principal:

> It was encouraging to note the energy and resourcefulness of your students and staff alike. Apart from the spirit of self-help, which was evident at your school, I wish to emphasise that discipline and organisation must indeed be

Chapter 11 – 'Energy and resourcefulness'

encouraged, as these are the basis of leadership training. It was therefore gratifying to note that these have been given some prior attention at your school.[1]

If President Kaunda saw the urgent need for leadership training at this stage of his country's history, Bishop Furstenberg was also aware of it. It might be said that his regular attendance at Vatican II sessions from 1962 to 1965 gave fresh impetus to his outstanding pastoral commitment to the diocese of Mbala. He would have been familiar with the great document, *Gaudium et Spes*, known as *The Pastoral Constitution on the Church in the Modern World*, 8 December, 1965. This inspirational document delineates the solidarity of the Church with the whole of humanity. Its opening words were addressed to all people:

> The joy and hope, the grief and anguish of the people of our time, especially those who are poor or afflicted in any way, are the joy and hope, the grief and anguish of the followers of Christ as well.[2]

The closing of the Council, 8 December, 1965, coincided with new projects for training in leadership and community development initiated by the new Zambian government. Centres for these projects were springing up throughout the country. The Bishop was quick to take the lead in providing the first Community Development Centre in the township of Abercorn (Mbala). As early as 1962, he had approached Mother Antonia for a Sister to help local women "to run their little homes".[3] In May 1965, he reported to Mother Antonia that Sister Patricia McNulty was running the Centre "with great success". With his eye characteristically on the future, he pointed out the need for development in this area. The Bishop reported to Mother Bernadette:

> As long as the course is only for women in the Mbala township Sr. Patricia can cope very well alone, but on the next Four-Year-Development Plan, starting July 1966, a Housecraft Training Centre is foreseen. This Centre is to train leaders for Women's Clubs all over the District. Once the District Training Centre comes into being Sr. Patricia will need help. I would be very grateful if you could foresee a Sister for this. It would be ideal if she had a degree. But the present government does not insist on the degree. Experience would be sufficient or she could follow a short course in Community Development.[4]

Sister Patricia's small beginnings at Mbala had important implications for the future. Once she had trained sufficient Zambian leaders, she was able to move on during the 1970s to a larger training project at Mpika, near Chilonga/Lwitikila.

Alongside Education and Training in Leadership, standards of health care had greatly improved in the new foundation at Chilonga. This grant-aided Mission Hospital had a certain degree of freedom to draw on donations and gifts to enhance facilities and equipment. The four S.R.N. Sisters employed in the government hospital at Mbala did not enjoy the same privileges under the administration of the Ministry of Health, and were subject to government regulations.

A letter of thanks written by the Sisters of Chilonga to the Congregation in the U.K., Ireland and California, reflects what had been accomplished during the first ten years of the hospital's existence:

> Our hospital here comprises the following: two medical wards, two surgical wards, one children's ward, one isolation block, one maternity block, an out-patients' department, a theatre, an X-ray department. We have a daily av-

erage of one hundred and twenty-five patients in the wards, and one hundred and fifty out-patients. Trainee nurses, who are under the supervision and guidance of our own Sisters, give nursing care to these patients. All theory is given to the students in the classroom and demonstration room by Sister Josephine.[5]

At this stage, the level of secondary education in Zambia was basic. Entrants to the Nursing School were expected to have reached Standard Six (top class Primary School), or Form Two of Secondary School. Once students had completed the three-year course at Chilonga, they were awarded the certificate of a Zambian Enrolled Nurse, equivalent to that of a State Enrolled Nurse (S.E.N.) in the U.K. The Sisters at Chilonga wrote: "These nurses do wonderful work and help the suffering people enormously".[6]

In 1966, Zambia had only one training school for Registered Nurses at Kitwe, where entry required G.C.S.E. qualification (Form Five) as in the U.K. or the Irish Leaving Certificate. The Chilonga Sisters noted:

> It will be many years before the country is able to produce enough S.R.N.S to serve this vast territory. At least we feel we are helping in a small way to relieve the sufferings of the people.[7]

In 1965, the Chilonga Hospital was also recognised as a training school for Enrolled Midwives. This course lasted one year and usually followed on from the general course for Enrolled Nurses. The Sisters wrote:

> This midwifery training is particularly important to us as the standard of midwifery in Zambia is so low – no antenatal clinics and no hospitals within a radius of 150 miles.

> The maternal and infancy mortality rates are extremely high as a result. Our aim is to train these nurses in midwifery and place them in clinics up and down the country, and in this way we will be in a position, by examination of the patient, to detect any abnormalities and to bring the mother to the hospital. The government has already set up many clinics, but at the present time there are no trained midwives to fill the posts.[8]

Towards the 1970s, the hospital continued to expand. A new government gave a grant of seventy-five per cent for another extension, the diocese of Mbala contributing the remainder. Bedding and equipment were supplied by private donations from benefactors in Germany, the U.K. and Ireland. Despite the heavy demands for ongoing funding for mission foundations, the Sisters in the Mother House at Chigwell continued financial support, especially for the purchase of heavy equipment such as ambulances and motor vehicles, so that the hospital could serve a wide outreach in remote areas in the bush. It was not uncommon for the Sisters and their helpers to bring gravely ill patients, including mothers and babies, along hazardous bush tracks for treatment in the hospital.

The pastoral needs of patients were met by the White Fathers

> who have long ago won the confidence of the people. They come to the wards each evening to comfort and help the sick.[9]

Whenever the priests themselves were in need of hospital care, they were accommodated either in the private wing or in the visitors' room in the convent. Going 'on tour' for several weeks to celebrate the Eucharist and administer the Sacraments to the people in remote villages, exposed them to a variety of harmful diseases, especially malaria. Their mode of transport was usually a motorbike, and this involved manoeuvring bumpy, difficult terrain. The missionaries were well acquainted with the customs and traditions of the people. In the field of medicine, they were not without knowledge of cures for minor illnesses, always carrying around with them *'muti'* or medicine boxes containing items such as quinine for alleviating the symptoms of malaria. The people regarded the priests as their friends, who would assist them not only spiritually, but also restore them to physical health.

After the departure of Dr. Wheeler and his family to the U.S.A., the hospital was fortunate to obtain the services of a young woman doctor from Germany, Bernadina Fueurborne. She had been recruited by Bishop Furstenberg. The Sisters described her in one of their letters as "completely dedicated to the patients".[10] She was a gifted physician and surgeon and despite limited resources, performed many successful operations. She worked closely with the Northern Provincial Medical Officer, Dr. Derek Braithwaite, who had long medical experience in the territory and who piloted his own plane in emergencies. Dr. Fueurborne earned the trust of the Zambian people by her humanity, kindness and compassion. Her green 'Beetle' Volkswagen was a familiar sight in and around the bush roads of Chilonga and Mpika.

The support staff at Chilonga came mainly from the German voluntary organisation 'Misereor', already referred to. This organisation supplied a steady stream of highly-skilled young people. The Pathology Laboratory technician, Hildegarde, provided an invaluable service identifying tropical and other diseases. A group of nurses also came from this organisation. Elizabeth is remembered for her devotion to and care of the sick. The mission's electricity was supplied by a generator set up by Anton and was limited to two hours every evening. In order to perform operations during the day, it was necessary to activate the generator and this was managed by other electricians such as Rudi Adler or other Misereor volunteers. It was Anton (now Fr. Anton) who installed electricity in the entire missions of Chilonga and Lwitikila.

As already mentioned, Chilonga Hospital was ideally situated on the Great North Road, near the junction with the Kasama/Mbala road. Even in the first years of its existence, it served numerous long-distance travellers who were involved in accidents, or people who wished to stop on their journey to Dar-es-Salaam on the east coast, or on their way to Lake Tanganika in the north. The hospital frequently served the needs of large international work forces that came to set up the country's infra-structure. Among these were Canadian engineers who laid the much-needed oil pipeline from the east coast of Tanzania to the Copperbelt in Zambia, and later on to the team that built the railway along a similar route.

The Chilonga Maternity Wing was the birthplace of many children. Some of the young mothers who were teaching at Lwitikila School had their babies there. Benedict John (Ben) James, second child of Mary and Patrick James, was born there on 12 January, 1966, and, with his brother John, spent his early childhood playing in the spacious campus of Lwitikila School. Dr. Fueurbome and a team of five midwives were available to assist delivery. Francis, the first child of Catherine and Michael Davis, was born there on 5 March, 1967. These young children brought a joyful, happy dimension to life on the mission. In recent years, Ben and Francis revisited their birthplace and found few changes at Chilonga![11]

Within the brief space of ten years, the shared vision of Bishop Joseph Van den Biesen and Mother Antonia had become a reality. Their dream in 1955 to have a hospital to serve the people in this remote part of Africa might be said to have been an act of faith at the time it was conceived, but, as the poet W.B. Yeats reminds us, a dream can be a lasting inspiration:

I have spread my dreams under your feet
Tread softly because you tread on my dreams.[11]

NOTES
1. Pope John XXIII. *Address on the Convocation of the Second Vatican Council*, Rome: 29 Dec, 1961.
2. *Gaudium et Spes*. Document. Second Vatican Council, Rome: 1965.
3. Furstenberg, Bishop A. *Letter to Mother Antonia, Zambia:* 12 Aug., 1963.
4. ibid. 19 Aug., 1963.
5-9. Sisters of the Chilonga Community. *Letter to the Congregation to celebrate 10 years in Chilonga:* New Year, 1966.
10. Davis, Francis. *Revisiting Chilonga*. (undated)
11. Yeats, W.B. "He wishes for the cloth of Heaven", *Collected Poems*, Wordsworth Press: London, p. 59.

CHAPTER 12

Exploring the New Ways

POPE JOHN XXIII is said to have referred to his calling of the Second Vatican Council (1962-1965) as the opening of a window to allow a breath of fresh air through the Church.[1] Some commentators, however, have frequently compared it to a 'hurricane', so great were the changes ushered in by the Council. These changes were felt throughout the entire Church, not least within Religious Orders and Congregations. The Council issued a special decree, *Perfectae Cantatas*, 29 October, 1965, setting out the renewal of Religious Life. Quoting from *Lumen Gentium* (the Dogmatic Constitution of the Church, November, 1964) the Council Fathers confirmed that Religious Life "traced its origins to the teaching and example of the Divine Master" and stated that it is a very clear symbol of the heavenly kingdom. The more fervently, therefore, the more they [religious]

> join themselves with Christ, by the gift of their whole life, the fuller does the Church's life become and the more vigorous and fruitful its apostolate.[2]

Chapter 12 – Exploring the New Ways

All religious Orders and Congregations were urged towards

> a constant return to the sources of the Christian life and the primitive inspiration of the Institute, and their adaptation to the changed condition of our time.[3]

The spiritual renewal of each member was of paramount importance because without this any adaptation would be of no avail.

In contrast with their lives before Vatican II, Religious Orders were now directed to carry out renewal programmes themselves. Sufficient prudent experimentation was allowed and competent authorities, especially General Chapters, were to establish norms for renewal and legislate for them. Under Mother Etheldreda (Mary Gleeson, Superior General 1965-1978), the Sisters of the Sacred Hearts of Jesus and Mary held their first special Chapter in August, 1969. This was a time of unprecedented change and many Sisters were bewildered by the sudden unexpected sense of loss for long-held practices, now replaced by new, unfamiliar ones. Change affected their way of life, including prayer and the religious dress. Throughout the Church, there was an exodus of priests and religious who questioned their vocations and decided to return to the lay state. However, many religious, especially those in the younger age group, happily embraced the recommendations of Vatican II. They welcomed the new emphasis on personal responsibility, involvement in community decision-making, individual identity and the availability of more personal time and space.

The next General Chapter was held in Chigwell in July, 1972 and, according to Mother Etheldreda, the Sisters "re-edited and amended portions of the Declarations, Directives and Guidelines of the Special Chapter of 1969."[4]

The missions in Central Africa were also affected by changes in the Church in the aftermath of the Council. Here, too, shortages in personnel became acute when Sisters were withdrawn to replace those on the home mission who had left the Congregation or who had been sent on renewal courses. Some Sisters re-evaluated their ministries and pursued alternative apostolates. During this period, there was also a trend towards what was then called 'individual apostolates' as opposed to those carried out in institutions such as hospitals and schools.

The secondary school for girls at Lwitikila suffered severe setbacks in the 1970s, despite its ongoing success since its foundation in 1962. In 1973, Sister John Vincent resigned as head teacher and Sister Edmund Campion was appointed Acting Head in 1974. Sister Mary Costello opted to train in the U.K. as a Registered Nurse and Midwife, and returned to Zambia to serve in the Health Care ministry at a later date. Sister Scholastica (Bridget McCourt), Head of the Home Economics Department, was recalled in 1974 as her skills were urgently needed in the U.K. She was replaced by Sister Eileen Hennebry. Sister Mary Bosco, a retired head teacher in her 70s, became Superior of the Lwitikila Mission. Her love for the Zambian people was legendary.

As evident in its early history, Lwitikila was no stranger to tragedy. Another terrible blow struck in May, 1972 when Christine McDonald (niece of Sister John Vincent) was killed in a car accident on the Great North Road, near Serenje, on her return journey from Lusaka. Accompanied by Sister Amabilis, Sister John made the sad journey to Lusaka to travel with the remains back to her native South Uist in Scotland.[5] Christine had been Head of the History Department at the school and had set up a museum exhibiting artifacts of Zambian culture. Today it remains a poignant memorial to her young life cut short so tragically.

By the mid 1970s, Lwitikila school was giving cause for alarm. The Vicar General, Father Pascal Kakakota of the Mbala Diocese, wrote to Mother Etheldreda to inform her that

> according to the Provincial Inspector of Secondary Schools, this school was on the brink of collapsing.[6]

Father Kakakota also quoted Bishop Furstenberg, who had warned him that unless more Sisters were appointed "the school will face the great danger of going down in many respects."[7] There was a need for

> a nucleus of Sisters from the Congregation of the Sacred Hearts of Jesus and Mary, since the school had been entrusted to them.[8]

One can only imagine the dilemma facing Mother Etheldreda and the General Council on receiving this report. Sister Edmund Campion went home on leave in May, 1975 and was replaced by Sister Catherine Collins as acting head teacher in the same year.

While the school at Lwitikila struggled to survive, there were encouraging developments taking place fifteen miles away at Mpika. After Sister Patricia had trained Zambians to take over the first Training Centre at Mbala, she went to Mpika in 1975 to set up a similar centre for young girls. This was part of a training co-operative. The girls were taught cookery, needlework and mothercraft. The course lasted for one year, at the end of which girls were selected to work in commercial units of dressmaking and baking, which developed alongside training classes. Sister Patricia was assisted by Sister Devota, who had already been running two women's clubs in the area. The two Sisters drove every day to Mpika from Lwitikila Convent, where they resided.[9] This centre, sometimes known as the Self-Help Centre, was a very important beginning to what later grew into the Institute for Christian Leadership (I.C.L.). We can get a picture of the hard work done by Sisters Patricia and Devota in the early days of its existence in a letter of appreciation from Father Piwek, a founding member, to Mother Etheldreda, 28 March, 1976:

> Since the beginning of March forty-two teenage girls have started a six-month course. Sister Patricia has begun her work with great enthusiasm and efficiency. We are sure that the homecraft centre will be the best section in the Co-operative. Sister Ellen (Burke) also comes twice in the week to help in the kitchen, and when she comes very tasty things are produced which immediately attract many customers.
>
> After six months the more successful girls will start work in the Commercial Unit. Our aim is to build up a community-based and self-financed training centre for young people. Zambia is in great need of exploring new ways in this direction. We are very glad that we are now able to train young girls as well as boys. The Church in this country, after concentrating so long on its traditional social engagements in hospitals and schools, is now trying new ways to help the people.[10]

These early beginnings of the Institute for Christian Leadership were to play a significant part in the ongoing development of the country as a whole, as will be seen at a later stage. The project was the first of its kind in Zambia.

Throughout the 1970s, the Health Care ministry initiated by the Sisters in the 1970s made remarkable progress. Several Sisters, most of whom were Registered Nurses and Midwives from the U.K. and Ireland, played their part in raising health care standards in Mbala and Chilonga, in the Northern Province. They built on the solid foundations laid by the early Sisters – Sisters Kieran Marie, Mary of the Sacred Heart, La Salette, John Baptist, Canice, Josephine, Catherine Kennedy and Francis Jerome McCarthy. Following in their footsteps, Sister Celine de Jesu O'Keefe recorded her own account of her assignment to Chilonga Mission in October, 1971. She wrote:

> While I was in South Uist N.H.S. Hospital I was assigned to Zambia as midwifery tutor in the midwifery unit at our mission hospital. We departed from Heathrow Airport on 15th October at 21.00 hours. It was a strange experience, the first of many to come. As we flew out into the very dark sky the soft sound of the song "Ramona, I hear the mission bells are calling" rang out in the Zambian Airways flight to Lusaka.[11]

After completing her 400 miles trek along the Great North Road to her destination at Chilonga, Sister Celine described her first impressions of the place:

> My first introduction to the hospital was like leafing through the pages of a medical book. It was all there to be seen: schismosomiasis, trypanosomiasis, kwashiorkor, the fevered brow of the malaria patient and bare-ribbed pot-bellied child with hookworm disease. Harrowing to see, a lot to study. In the maternity unit at least I could feel at home. The good Lord made all colours and creeds the same. With a stethoscope, blood pressure apparatus and thermometer I could get on with my work, regardless of language. Of course the students knew English from study for their Enrolled General Nursing qualifications.[12]

A very important part of the Sisters' health care service was its outreach to the villages within reasonable access to the hospital. The fourteen original outreach clinics increased to twenty-five. Sister Celine gives an interesting account of what this service involved:

> These were commonly known as outreach clinics. Their main purpose was to administer the vaccines to the children for the prevention of diseases and to check the antenatal patients for admission to the hospital. Each child was visited once a month by the team led by a nurse, the Health Education Officer, (who would give a talk to the people), and three student nurses, one of whom would prepare a talk on a medical condition. Health education was very important.[13]

The risks incurred by team members on these medical 'missions' were clearly delineated by Sister Celine when she recorded the experience:

> The team would set off at 7.00 hours in a four wheeled automobile, equipped with all the requisites for the day, returning at 18.00 tired but happy. The most difficult clinic to reach was in the Luangwa Valley. It could only be accessed three times in the dry season (April – October), just enough time to give the vaccines to the children. The remainder of the year the route was impassable.
>
> The Luangwa Valley lies to the east of Chilonga (Mpika) and extends south to Kapata. Along the course of the river it forms the boundary with Malawi. It is the second largest National Park in Africa for the preservation of wildlife and considered a unique example of the 'real Africa'. The north being in the Mpika district, was within our area for outreach work. Patients from there would come to the hospi-

Chapter 12 – Exploring the New Ways

tal for treatment, despite the hazardous route. It was very difficult driving to the clinic, no road, only rock tracks, holes and boulders to be negotiated. At one point, when crossing the river the team had to disembark and wade across lest the vehicle got stuck in the river bed.

All the sick children would arrive at the health centre and receive treatment and the children were vaccinated. The team would stay overnight, the men would sleep in the automobile and the ladies on the floor of the centre. The expatriates enjoyed going to this clinic despite the hardships involved especially the extreme heat of the valley. The game reserve was a special attraction. Hippotami in large numbers could be seen in the river, and crocodiles lazed on its banks. Animals such as buffalo, monkeys, baboons and a variety of antelope could be seen at close range, not to mention the magnificent birds. Altogether a memorable experience in the wilds of the beautiful Luangwa Valley acclaimed in prose and poetry by Ernest Hemmingway, though danger loomed at every angle. The team was sometimes greeted by Chief Luangwa, who was often encouraged by the District Officer at Mpika to leave the valley with his community to reside in a safer area, but he always refused.[14]

In the early seventies there were significant changes in the day-to-day running of Chilonga Hospital. After the departure of Dr. Fueurborne to her native Germany, the hospital was administered by three doctors recruited by an agency, Medicus Mundi, in Belgium, Holland and Germany. This agency faithfully sent doctors and surgeons on three or six-year contracts. A month before a contract expired, a replacement doctor arrived. Houses for doctors and medical staff were built within easy access to the hospital. As the number of beds increased, (Mpika was an expanding township), more qualified nursing staff were needed. Some of these came from organisations in the U.K. and Ireland, for example, the Voluntary Service Overseas (V.S.O.). Working alongside the young Zambian student nurses, these professionals ensured that the highest standards of care were maintained.

Despite the advances made at the hospital, the health of mothers and babies remained critical and infant mortality was still very high. Sister Celine gives a clear picture of the situation from her own experience:

> My work in the midwifery ward was very interesting, very different from that in Europe because of the complications. I admitted a lady one morning at 8.30. She had walked eight miles from Mufubushi. By 11.00 am she was the mother of triplets. No incubator. It was the rainy season, drying so much baby clothes was a problem to be surmounted, and also the need for baby-bottles and baby-food. It was necessary to keep them for six weeks. And the mother, so anxious to get home, had to stay until they were fit for discharge. She had eight children, a change to eleven was not easy. She was allowed home with two, Vitaliano and Regina. Cephas, the smallest, we kept for another month. She arrived on the day he was ready to go. If we had lived in a part of the developed world we would have been a subject for the media. They were checked regularly at the under-fives clinic, and made good progress. The mother returned with them when they made their First Holy Communion and they were three lovely healthy children.[15]

Transporting patients, especially in the remote bush areas, was a continual problem. Villages were mostly situated at a distance from the roadside. The driver had to wait until relatives led the way along a path through the bush. The patient was

Chapter 12 – Exploring the New Ways

then carried by helpers to the waiting vehicle. A torch was essential, especially at night, and also to light up the dimly-lit hut. Chilonga Hospital provided an on-call midwifery service at night, which Sister Celine recalls:

> The person on call would put a small red lamp on her window for the night watchman to identify the room and deliver the message. There was, as yet, no electricity in the rural areas. We had a small generator which supplied a few bulbs to the hospital, and a smaller one used in emergencies in the operating theatre. At night, if called, one would walk through the garden, a pleasant experience in the clear bright light of the moon and the cloudless starry sky, the distinctive constellation, the Southern Cross visible to the south. The perfume from the flowers and trees, especially the Frangipani, filled the warm air. So very pleasant that the tiredness would disappear. But a rather different experience in the rainy season.[16]

Towards the end of the 1970s, the Zambian Minister of Health initiated the Primary Health Care programme. The slogan 'Health for All by 2000' was posted everywhere. It meant that everyone would be within easy reach of a well-staffed rural health centre or hospital, where they could receive treatment and hopefully make a quick recovery. The health programme for the Zambian people had been envisaged for a long time by the Sisters of the Sacred Hearts of Jesus and Mary, and also by other medical mission providers such as the Irish Sisters of Charity, the Holy Rosary Sisters (Killashandra), and the Franciscan Sisters of the Divine Motherhood, all of whom had been working towards this goal for several decades. With their various levels of medical expertise, the Sisters now collaborated to ensure that the programme got off to a good start, many of them playing a leading role in setting up and delivering new health care curricula.

Long before the *Decree on Ecumenism* was proclaimed by the Second Vatican Council, 21 November, 1964, missionaries were actively engaged in dialogue with members of other churches. This was happening almost imperceptibly in the fields of medicine and health care, fulfilling, without being aware of it, the opening aspiration of the Council itself:

> The restoration of unity among Christians is one of the principal concerns of the Second Vatican Council.[17]

This quotation could well be applied to the ministries carried out at Lwitikila, Mpika, Chilonga and Mbala, where there were no boundaries separating one faith from another. In addition to members of the Catholic Church, all the main religions in Zambia were catered for: Anglicans, United Church of Zambia, Seventh Day Adventists, Jehovah's Witnesses, Christ Church Scientists, Muslims. Lwitikila and Chilonga were both diocesan foundations and their mission was to uphold sound Christian principles. Their missionary endeavours are clearly reflected in these words from the decree on Ecumenism:

> These communions [denominations] engage in their more intensive cooperation in carrying out any duties for the common good of humanity which are demanded by every Christian conscience.[18]

The changes in the universal Church which took place in the 1970s had far-reaching effects, particularly in Africa. The emphasis on institutional missionary work (hospitals and schools) now changed to an apostolate which embraced outreach clinics and self-help groups. This would eventually lead to leadership training, thus preparing Zambian youth to become conscientious and efficient leaders of their country.

NOTES

1-2.	*Perfectae Caritatis.* Rome: para. 1
3.	ibid, para.2.
4.	Mother Etheldreda. *Circular Letter to the Sisters of the Congregation,* Chigwell: 20 Aug., 1978.
5.	Hennessy, Sr. Amabilis. *Obituary for Christine MacDonald,* Lwitikila: May. 1972.
6-8.	Kakakota, Father P. *Letter to Rev. Mother Ethedreda,* Bishop's House, Mbala: 2 July, 1974.
9.	Piwek, Fr. U. *Letter to Sr. Austin,* Zambia: 28 Mar., 1976.
10.	ibid. *Email to Sr. Austin,* Germany: 18 July, 2012.
11-16.	O'Keefe, Sr. Celine de Jesu. *Account of my Zambian Sojourn,* Cork: Sept. 2012.
17.	*Decree on Ecumenism.* Rome: 24 Nov. 1964. para. 1.
18.	ibid. para. 4.

CHAPTER 13

Reading the Signs of the Times

IN THE VATICAN II DOCUMENT, *Perfectae Caritatis*, religious orders were directed to

> a constant return to the sources of the Christian life and to the primitive aspirations of the Institutes... by accepting and retaining the spirit of the Founder.[1]

The Sisters of the Sacred Hearts of Jesus and Mary reverted to mid-nineteenth century France and England to rediscover the charism of their Founder, Father Victor Braun.[2] This charism was an apostolate to marginalised and underprivileged people, especially women and children. Father Braun would have felt at home in mid-twentieth century Central Africa, where his spirit continued wherever the Sisters served in the healing and education ministries. These ministries were to expand and become more diversified in the years ahead.

The Sisters in Zambia were formed into a region in 1978, with Sr. Cyril McCormick as Regional Superior. Under her leadership, the Sisters faced the difficulties of the 1980s. This was a time when Zambia suffered the effects of currency devaluation and world debt and this resulted in extreme poverty and food scarcity. Hospitals were severely understaffed and underfunded and this created much unrest and disquiet among the people. Within the Congregation itself there were also concerns, in common with all religious orders at that time, that fewer young women were entering novitiates in Ireland and Britain. The Sisters in these countries were stretched to their limits in order to sustain their apostolates at home. Nevertheless, their generosity and spirit of sacrifice with regard to the African Missions continued, not only in terms of financial support, but also in sending qualified personnel. In 1986, in Chilonga hospital alone, the Sisters in posts of responsibility were:

Sister Josephine Guiry	Matron
Sister Aidan Wall	Theatre Superintendent
Sister Rosalie Dunne	Director, School of Midwifery
Sister Celine O'Keefe	Director, School of General Nursing
Sister Kathleen Laverty	Ward Sister, Obstetrics
Sister Angela Rancalli	Ward Sister, Paediatrics[3]

Sister Oliver (Superior General) ensured that there were sufficient competent staff to maintain the fast-developing projects in Zambia. She believed that under the teaching and guidance of the Sisters and the expatriate professionals working alongside them, the young trainee nurses would be adequately qualified and eventually would be able to undertake the running of the hospital themselves.

A variety of undertakings were initiated under Sister Cyril's leadership. To celebrate the International Year of the Child, proclaimed by U.N. Secretary General, Kurt Waldheim, the Sisters at Chilonga set up five new outreach clinics specially equipped to cater for children from the pre-natal stage until the age of five years. Sister Cyril referred to this project in a letter:

> The growth of these clinics is proof of the dedication of the hospital staff to the improvement of childcare for as many children as possible, in as wide an area as possible.[4]

Her words were echoed by President Kaunda himself in *Letter to My Children*:

> You have been born in an age which offers greater opportunities for personal fulfilment and human service than any other which preceded it.[5]

The Silver Jubilee of the Sisters' arrival in Zambia in 1956 was celebrated at Chilonga on 9 October, 1981. Sister Cyril described the occasion as "truly brilliant".[6] The Thanksgiving Mass for twenty-five years of dedicated service was concelebrated by Bishop Furstenberg of Mbala and Bishop Mutale of Kasama, Sister Oliver, and her Assistant, Sr. Laura Ryan, came from Chigwell for the occasion. Sister Cyril wrote:

> The throbbing drums, the enthusiastic singing of the children from the local school, the happy shining faces of the large congregation filled one with deep joy.[7]

Chilonga Hospital itself continued to become even busier, not only with patients from its surrounding area, but because of the accidents resulting from an increase in heavy traffic on the pot-holed Great North Road. Emergency cases were not uncommon. Long-distance lorry drivers, transporting goods to and from Dar-es-Salaam in Tanzania, faced huge hazards, especially after 6.00 p.m., in the heat and darkness of the rainy season. It was not unusual to see an overturned vehicle on the roadside, perhaps overloaded or badly loaded, with its contents strewn on the road. Food items were picked up by nearby villagers. During the early 1980s, there were two major acci-

Chapter 13 – Reading the Signs of the Times

dents in two years near the hospital. In both cases, a bus overturned. Sister Celine described the horrific scene of one of these accidents:

> There were nine fatalities. Every doctor and nurse on the campus worked through the night to deal with the injuries, major and minor, intravenous infusions, painkillers, plaster of Paris and bandages applied. All worked quietly and quickly. The Flying Doctor Service was called to transport cases to Ndola. The neighbourhood was in shock. In the event of future major accidents the doctors (all of them Europeans) asked us to draw up a disaster plan as soon as possible.[8]

Zambia was a young nation and it was to be expected that it had a Government policy to indigenise all leadership posts in the country. The University of Zambia had been founded as late as 1965 and the number of trained graduates for these posts was inadequate. The Catholic Church had been working towards preparing Zambian leaders for a number of years. The Junior Seminary at Lubushi and St. Dominic's Major Seminary in Lusaka continued to prepare young Zambian candidates for the priesthood. In 1987, the German Bishop of Mbala, Adolf Furstenberg, retired and was replaced by the Zambian Bishop, Telesphore Mpundu (now Archbishop of Lusaka).

The Sisters of the Sacred Hearts of Jesus and Mary were also playing their part in preparing personnel to direct the Mission Hospital at Chilonga. Since the hospital at Mbala was Government-owned, the question of indigenising posts did not arise. Sister Oliver, in collaboration with Sister Scholastica, Superior of the Zambian Sisters of the Child Jesus, arranged to send one of these Sisters, Sister Clementina, a Registered Nurse, to London for training in hospital administration.

It was hoped that she would eventually take over the management of Chilonga Hospital. In the meantime, the Sisters of the Sacred Hearts would continue to work in different posts of responsibility. Changes would take time and they would have to wait patiently.

The appointment of a Zambian head teacher at Lwitikila School proved problematic and was a matter of concern for Sister Cyril and the Sisters. Mr. Mpondi had been appointed Head in 1978 but his time in this post was short-lived. By 1983, Sister Catherine Collins was still Acting head teacher, with Mr. Mapani as Deputy Head. The Minutes of the Area Meeting, 14 January, 1984, indicate that "Sister Catherine Collins is aware of filling in until a suitable Zambian Head can be found"[9] It would appear from this meeting that the appointment posed a dilemma for the Sisters judging from a remark that

> It has been said by Father Vincent, Education Secretary, Catholic Secretariat, Lusaka, that there was no one suitable to take on this position.[10]

Indigenisation raised many questions for the Congregation at home and on the missions. Had we adequately prepared young Zambians for posts of responsibility in our schools and hospitals? Are our Sisters still needed in the fields of education and health care? If so, what should be their role? Did indigenisation mean that the Sisters could now go home? What were the greatest needs to be met by the Sisters, considering their abilities and health? The general response to these questions was that they should remain on the missions in a supportive role. It would take time to replace the Sisters in the Midwifery and Nursing Schools and to appoint Senior Ward Sisters. Most Sisters agreed that they should not abandon the apostolate they had begun twenty-five years previously. There were other urgent needs to be met, such as the education and care of children with special needs, caring for the sick in their own homes (home-based care), greater focus on mothers and babies and further involvement in Leadership Training at the Institute for Christian Leadership at Mpika.[11] These questions were discerned by the Congregation in the light of the Founder's charism and in reading the signs of the times.

Within a short time, the Sisters discovered where many of their future apostolates would be. In the mid 1980s, world scientists were struggling to isolate the causative organism, Pyrexia of unknown origin. This 'new disease' did not respond to any known medication and caused general sickness and many deaths. Eventually, the Human Immune Deficiency Virus (HIV) was discovered and this resulted in the terminal illness, Acquired Immune Deficiency Syndrome (AIDS). Although the disease became a global phenomenon, the most seriously affected part of the world was Sub-Saharan Africa. Sister Celine wrote of her own experience in Chilonga:

> This caused havoc in the country. As people were poor and undernourished, they quickly reached the terminal stage of the infection, there was no medication or vaccine, hospitals and clinics became overcrowded, reaching crisis point. Eventually a system of home-based care was introduced whereby terminally ill patients were nursed in their own homes. Sister Romana (Rita Hennessy) and Sister Catherine Kennedy became known as 'the Angels of Chilonga' because of their continuous care of the sick and dying in the town and in the surrounding villages. The people were depressed and angry with the Government, a lot of unrest.[12]

The AIDS pandemic gave rise to a change of direction in the Congregation's health care mission in Zambia. In relation to this, some of the Nursing Sisters, notably the late Sister Rosalie Dunne, initiated and sustained a variety of projects, each one remarkable in itself.

After the General Chapter at Chigwell in August, 1984, Sister John Vincent succeeded Sr. Cyril as the Regional Superior in Zambia. She had been in the country since 1963 and was aware of the need to train young people for leadership roles. Her work at the Institute of Christian Leadership at Mpika included training Parish Co-ordinators and Parish Sisters. This was a time when the laity were becoming more involved in parish work. Sr. John Vincent was principally involved in running courses for Resource Teachers, helping them to become more self-reliant. She also trained local girls from Sr. Patricia's staff to become leaders of various women's groups in the Diocese.[13]

Sr. Oliver was acutely aware of the need for care of Zambian children with disabilities. In September, 1985, she commissioned the late Sr. Mary Angela Long to write a report on the provision of Special Educational Needs in the country.[14] Sr. Mary Angela had been head of a school in Ireland for children with mild to severe disabilities. Her report followed the U.N. Declaration of the International Year for Disabled Persons by the U.N. Secretary General, Kurt Waldheim, in 1981, and the National Commission in Zambia launched by President Kaunda in 1983. One of the projects adopted by the Commission was the National Campaign to Reach Disabled Children. Phase One of the campaign was carried out by a multi-disciplinary team from the Ministries of Education and Culture, Health and Labour and Social Services, with the support of UNICEF. The team worked for six months, from 1982 to 1983, collecting and examining data from children who had been registered. All the children were between five and fifteen years old.

In her report, Sr. Mary Angela quotes from a Paper given by Professor Serpen of Zambia University at the Nairobi Conference, November, 1982:

> In the newly independent nations of Africa the extent of services for the education and rehabilitation of disabled children of all types is severely limited and is especially inadequate for the mentally handicapped.[15]

Sister Angela's study was confined to the Northern Province where she found that there were few if any services available for the mentally handicapped. She discovered in statistics from the Province that of the 880 children examined only 25 were considered handicapped.

> It would seem probable that some of the 37 registered as having multiple handicap, as well as the 189 registered as physically handicapped could also have severe learning problems and consequently be termed mentally handicapped.[16]

Sr. Mary Angela recommended a 'community-based approach' towards educating children with special needs. The classes in the schools had an average of 60 pupils, much too large to enable these children to receive the attention they needed. She highlighted the urgency for a change in attitudes towards disability. Most importantly, she pointed out that a number of children in Africa suffered permanent physical damage as a result of T.B., measles, whooping cough, polio and osteomyelitis, all of which were preventable with immunisation. The declaration in 1983 by the World Health Organisation of the Year of African Immunisation was welcome news. The effectiveness of the immunisation programme would determine whether some Zambian children could live a normal life or go through life with a disability which could have been prevented. Sr. Mary Angela concluded her report on an optimistic note:

> Zambia's strong family tradition, the respect and love given to the old, are positive indicators for the future of a programme of care and education for children with disabilities.[17]

Bishop Furstenberg of Mbala, in whose diocese Sr. Mary Angela carried out her study, approached Sister Oliver and Sister John Vincent with a view to setting up a special school for deaf children in his diocese. Sister Mary Costello, who had been a nurse and midwife at the Mbala Government Hospital from 1981-1984, agreed to undertake this ground-breaking apostolate. She had already been a Maths teacher in the early days of Lwitikila School. Her new assignment, however, required specialised training at Hertfordshire College, Watford, U.K. By the time she arrived back in Zambia, September, 1987, a new government policy for the Education of the Deaf had been introduced. Schools for the deaf were no longer considered the best way forward and units for the deaf in primary schools were recommended. Sr. Mary Costello initiated a School Health Service in the Mbala district as a starting point. She describes what this involved:

> Ear examination was an essential part of the programme and gave the opportunity to identify deaf children As my contract was with the Mbala diocese, my remit was to cover all districts in that diocese, Mbala, Chinsali, Mpika, Isoko, Nankonde, Serenji and part of Kasama – a very wide area.[18]

There were five main parts in her project:
1. School visits in collaboration with the local health centre, where children were examined and treated for ear diseases
2. Identifying deaf children
3. Finding teachers who were prepared to undertake specialist training for teaching deaf children
4. Setting up clinics in places where there was a concentration of deaf children
5. Follow-up of the children and support of these units

This work continued from 1987 until 1995. From the outset, all these units were part of the Ministry of Education system, with teachers on the government payroll. Sister Mary worked as a volunteer. Funding for the construction of the units came from Irish Aid. The Commonwealth Society for the Deaf in London also gave support and donated valuable equipment such as hearing aids. Five units had been set up by 1995 and they continue to provide services for deaf children up to the present day.

The Minutes of the Regional Meeting of the Sisters in Zambia, October, 1985, reflect a trend among the Sisters to see themselves within the wider context of the Church and the World. Despite the drop in vocations, there was a spirit of hope and optimism as they looked at new ways of spreading the apostolate foreseen by the Founder and "being ourselves examples of his compassion and concern for the poor."[19] Among the many issues discussed was one which the Congregation had occasionally highlighted but never decided on: Are we ready to admit young Zambian women into the congregation? The fifteen Sisters present at this meeting were asked to make a decision. Some were of the opinion that we should take Zambian postulants at this stage in order to continue the spirit of the Founder.

Others asked if, considering the age range of the Sisters in the Congregation, there would be a sufficient number of Sisters able and willing to offer training and formation within a time-span of twenty to thirty years. This question would be given serious consideration in the General Chapter of 1990.

Rapid changes in Africa in general and in Zambia in particular were a feature of the early 1980s. The challenge for the Congregation in Zambia was to accept and adapt to these changes. This was not an easy task and it was made all the more difficult by the decline in vocations to the religious life and also the politics in Post-Independent Zambia and true to the charism of our Founder, the Sisters met these challenges with fortitude and a spirit of sacrifice, so that a new and diversified apostolate came into being.

NOTES
1. Vatican Council II. *Perfectae Caritatis*. Rome: 19, para. 1.
2. Gallagher, Sr. Austin. "Father Vincent Braun and the Catholic Church in England and Wales 1870-1882", *Recusant Journal*, London: Oct., 2007.
3. Corbett, Sr. Angelo Roncalli. *Article. Chiionga Hospital*, London: 2011. p. 1.
4. Donnelly, Sr. Cyril. *Keeping in Touch*, Chigwell: Spring, 1982.
5. Kaunda, President K. *Letter to My Children*. Lusaka, 1982.
6-7. Donnelly, Sr. Cyril. *Letter to Sr. Oliver, Superior General*, Zambia: 9 Oct., 1991.
8. O'Keefe, Sr. Celine de Jesu. *Early Days at Chiionga* Chiionga: Chiionga: 1989.
9-10. *Minutes of Meeting*, Secondary School, Lwitikila: 14 Jan. 1984.
11. Long, Sr. Mary Angela. *Report on Special Needs in Zambia*, Mpika: 1984.
12. O'Keefe, Sr. Celine, op.cit.
13. *Minutes of Regional Meeting*, Chiionga: 1985. 14-17 Long, Sr. Mary Angela, op.cit.
14. Costello, Sr. Mary. *Report on Ministry to Deaf Children*, Zambia: 1987.
15. *Minutes of Regional Meeting*, op.cit.

CHAPTER 14

Handing Over

One sows, another reaps.
(John 4:13)

BY THE MID-EIGHTIES, the ministries performed by the Sisters in the Zambian region were becoming more diversified. Sister John Vincent McDonald was elected Regional Superior in 1984 and she took the view that despite the reduced number of Sisters in the region, there were many more urgent needs to be met. The government hospital at Mbala now had a lay Zambian administrator, with Sisters Cyril, Romana, Catherine Kennedy and Mary Costello on the staff. At an area meeting held on 18 October, 1986, Sister John Vincent invited the thirteen Sisters present to explore the following topics: The Charism of the Congregation, The Needs of Contemporary Zambia, Zambian Aspirants, Retirement, Elderly and Sick Sisters, New Forms of Community, The Financial State of the Region. The question of Zambian Aspirants being admitted to the Congregation generated most debate among the group. One Sister felt that having an international novitiate "would just be a dream". The majority of the Sisters were of the opinion that this new venture required an enormous leap of

Faith, since our Congregation was not traditionally a missionary one:

> Earlier in 1986, the Superior General, Sister Oliver Kinnane, and her Assistant, Sister Laura Ryan, had already addressed some of these questions during their Visitation. No decision was taken to admit local aspirants. The Education Ministry at Lwitikila, however, posed problems – The school had begun in 1962 and Sister Oliver very reluctantly agreed to withdraw the last remaining teaching Sister, Sister Catherine Collins, who had been Acting Head for three years. Another Sister from the school, Sister Edmund Campion (Jory), became secretary to Bishop Mpundu of Mbala Diocese.'[1]

The new religious Congregation who undertook the administration of Lwitikila was the Servants of Mary Immaculate (SMI), whose provincial house was in Kasisi, Lusaka. They were familiarly known as the Kasisi Sisters. They were Polish in origin and had been enrolling local vocations since the early 1960s, some of whom were already on the staff of Lwitikila.[2] For three years they had shared the convent with the Sisters of the Sacred Hearts until 1989 when Sisters La Salette, John Vincent and Patricia moved to new ministries in Ndola, 350 miles away. As recorded earlier in this narrative, the education ministry at Lwitikila was a courageous venture by Mother Antonia in 1962. Recognising the dire need for the education of women in Africa, she was prepared to make any sacrifice towards that end. The Congregation was happy that the school had been entrusted to a Congregation of dedicated Sisters, who, to this day, continue to run a centre of excellence based on sound Christian principles.

Chapter 14 – Handing Over

On the occasion of the handing over of the convent and school, the Provincial Superior, Sister Irene Chowa SMI. wrote on 18 July, 1989:

> Lwitikila Girls' Secondary School owes you, the Sisters of the Sacred Hearts of Jesus and Mary, a debt of deep gratitude. It was one of the first and best secondary schools in Zambia as a result of the great dedication with which you worked for so many years.[3]

Referring to the part of the convent left vacant after the departure of the Sisters of the Sacred Hearts, Sister Irene added:

> It will not be empty for long since we are planning to send more of our Sisters to Lwitikila in years to come. Already at the end of this year we shall have two Sisters who are graduating, one from the University of Zambia and another from Nkrumah T.T.C. With God's help, there will no longer be a staff-housing problem in Lwitikila when a greater percentage of staff will consist of Sisters.[4]

The Institute for Christian Leadership (ICL) opened in 1985 and was directed by Sister John Vincent. It catered for a range of services, including Child-to-Child activities, Women and Children First, support for teachers and young unemployed people, resources for adult conferences and training for catechists. On the same campus, Sr. Patricia trained young women in housekeeping, home economics and dressmaking. In her letter to Bishop Mpundu, 7 July, 1989, Sr. John Vincent informed him that these services would be transferred to Ndola, where the Ministry of Education had extended 'a positive invitation' and where Bishop De Jong had provided "a well-placed and secure house for the convent."[5] This new foundation in the Copperbelt town of Ndola, with its large urban population, was to be the starting point of many more ministries. Uprooting from the well-established mission of Lwitikila was a daunting task. In this, the Sisters were generously helped by Sister Devota, who had previously established women's clubs at Mpika and Chikwanda. Now in her seventies, she was indefatigable. Sister Marie Louise, who had recently completed a hospital chaplaincy course at the University of San Francisco, added to the number in the Community. Her special skills made a unique contribution to the pastoral ministry.

As already pointed out, steps had been taken to Zambianise the hospital staff at Chilonga. In the 1984 General Chapter Report, Sister Oliver remarked:

> The Sister Matron at the hospital is training a Zambian Sister from the Congregation of the Child Jesus (CCJ) hopefully to replace her in an effort to Zambianise the hospital administration.[6]

This was a time when government contracts with medical staff were expiring and not being renewed. The Zambian Ministry of Health had begun to appoint Zambian-trained staff to the hospital. Sister Angelo Roncalli described the situation at the time:

> In April 1988, Sister Elizabeth Mooney (a qualified nurse and midwife) joined us and in 1991 Sister Celine O'Keefe returned to the U.K. leaving the post of Director of Nursing vacant. I was asked to take on this role and I returned to the U.K. to train as a nursing tutor at the University of Cardiff. I returned to Chilonga where Sister Celine initiated me into the post before she left for her vacation at home. My Assistant was Mary Lyons from Ireland who belonged to the APSO agency.[7]

Chapter 14 – Handing Over

In the meantime, Sister Clementina Chisula went to London to train in hospital administration. After almost fifty years since its foundation, there was every hope that the hospital would soon be directed by a Zambian Sister.

In common with all hospitals in Africa during the 1980s, Our Lady's, Chilonga, was overwhelmed by what became known as the scourge of the twentieth century, the HIV/AIDS pandemic. Sister Angelo Roncalli again wrote about the situation:

> The pandemic was quickly gathering pace in Zambia and our work-load soared with it. The T.B. Ward, which at one time was almost empty, now overflowed with patients. It impeded the progress of our Under Fives clinics. Medically and socially, these factors brought about a deterioration in working relationships, resulting in much heartache and tension in the workplace.[8]

If the 1980s in Zambia was a period to be remembered as one of depressing sadness, there were some rays of hope coming through the darkness. One historic event was the visit of Pope John Paul II, who came to Zambia in 1989. Sister Celine caught the mood of the people:

> It was a good time, it raised the doom and gloom, even if only for a short time. The reception and welcome were very well prepared, people were happy, so good to see smiles again, colourful banners and colourful chitenge skirts, song and dance, it was a good time even if short. The Pontifical Mass was celebrated at Kitwe, 150,000 people attended, and had a wonderful celebration indeed. They enjoyed Pope John Paul, he was lovely with them, as they sang and cheered him along in his popemobile.[9]

Another highlight of Sr. Oliver's last Visitation was the invitation of the President of Zambia to State House, Lusaka. Here, Dr. Kaunda warmly welcomed her with Sisters Laura, La Salette and Celine. The President thanked the Congregation for its work in Zambia over the years. Zambian humanism, he said, is based on the belief that man is made in the image of God, and therefore the best way to serve God is to serve man. He expressed a wish that we would continue to minister in Zambia, and that we would grow in numbers. Sister Oliver responded by reiterating that same hope and spoke of the growth and development she had seen over the years of visiting Zambia.[10]

The President was well-known to the Sisters. He came from Chinsali in the Northern Province. Some of his family had been educated at Lwitikiia Secondary School and his mother had been a patient at Chilonga on two occasions. Sister Celine remembered her "being cared for in the convent for privacy while her daughter stayed to cook and care for her."[11] In gratitude, the President presented the Matron, Sister John Baptist Kennedy, with a copy of his book, Kaunda on Violence, on which he inscribed:

> "Love and service to God is always rewarded with genuine happiness. For your part we shall always be grateful. Keep it up and remember to do so while smiling. God bless. KD."[12]

The last decade of the twentieth century heralded bewildering changes for the Sisters in the Zambian region. It deserves a separate story.

Chapter 14 – Handing Over

NOTES

1. *Minutes of the Regional Council Meeting,* Chilonga: 18 Oct., 1986.
2. Hinfekaar, H. *History of the Catholic Church in Zambia: 1896-1996,* Lusaka: Bookworld Publishers, 2004. p. 222.
3, 4. Chowa, Sr. Irene S.M.I. *Letter to the Sisters of the Sacred Hearts departing Lwitikiia,* Zambia: 18 July, 1989.
5, 6. Kinnane, Sr. Oliver. *Acts of the Chapter,* Chigwell: 1984.
7, 8. Corbett, Sr. Angelo Roncalli. *Article on Chilonga Hospital,* Archives, Chigwell: 1988.
9. O'Keefe, Sr. Celine de Jesu. *Memories of my Sojourn in Zambia,* Zambia: 1989.
10. "Sr. Oliver as Guest of President Kaunda". *Keeping in Touch,* Chigwell: Spring, 1988.
11. Sr. Celine O'Keefe. op.cit.
12. Kaunda, President Kenneth. Words inscribed on his book *Kaunda on Violence.* Gift to Sr. John Baptist (Clare Kennedy).

CHAPTER 15

Racing Towards the Finish

*"We will not be talking about withdrawing,
but of expanding."*
(Sister John Vincent)

AT THE GENERAL CHAPTER in Chigwell, July, 1990, Sister John Vincent was elected Superior General. She held this office until 2002, having been re-elected in 1996. After more than twenty years spent on the Zambian Mission, it came as no surprise that she directed the attention of the Congregation to the urgent needs of the people there. On the eve of the Chapter, 31 July, 1990, she stated in her Report on the Zambian region:

> If we are to welcome Zambian candidates into our Congregation, the problems that continually arise with regard to Mbala and Chilonga communities are seen in a completely new light. We will not be talking about withdrawing but of expanding.[1]

With a sense of urgency she remained true to this vision, wasting no time setting up Religious Vocations Programmes and initiating or consolidating projects for AIDS/HIV related issues. If the Congregation was no longer involved in mainstream schools in Zambia, there were plans for new forms of education in the Health Care Ministry. Sisters and Associates/Volunteers continued to come from the U.K. and Ireland, most of whom were nurses, midwives, counsellors and other health care professionals.

Sister Angelo Roncalli (Corbett), who at that time was Director of the School of Nursing at Chilonga, recalls the rapid changes taking place in the early 1990s:

> At our General Chapter in 1990, Sister John Vincent was elected Superior General. A period of major changes throughout the Congregation began. Changes were also accelerating at Our Lady's Hospital. Sister Clementina S.C.J. returned from London, having completed a Hospital Management Course. Sister Josephine Guiry had the task of inducting her into the role of Matron. This was a daunting challenge for Sister Clementina as the Chilonga site included the General Hospital, the Nursing and Midwifery Schools, a very busy Outreach Patients' Department and an even busier Outreach Programme, which included clinics for the Under-Fives. In addition to all these, there were the gardens, the chicken and fish farms and numerous other minor projects, looking back now, I feel the whole undertaking overwhelmed Sister Clementina right from the start.[2]

By 1990, the hospital, which had been built up by the Sisters of the Sacred Hearts over many years, had reached crisis point. More and more expatriate staff were returning home while the Zambian Government appointed more civil servants to the hospital. There were now more Sisters of the indigenous Congregations on the staff.

In a Circular Letter to the Congregation after the 1990 Chapter, Sister John Vincent addressed the problem of the decline in vocations to the Religious Life:

> We have decided to invite young women who show an interest in Religious Life, to work with us for a year. At the end of the year we shall have mutual evaluation to see the possibility of their becoming novices. We ask each Sister to take serious responsibility for a happy, prayerful life-witness, and an open, hospitable community. This we consider to be the most important form of Vocations Promotions. At the same time, we are using every other means to attract more people to share religious life with us to meet the increasing needs of the poor and suffering around us.[3]

In the same Circular Letter, she drew the attention of the Congregation to the urgent need to promote vocations in relation to the Zambian AIDS/HIV pandemic:

> As a result of the new pandemic situation we have moved gradually out of works which can be Zambianised in order to concentrate on people with AIDS related illnesses, since it is the work not so far undertaken by others. We realise we cannot cope with the AIDS pandemic alone so we have decided to meet the needs through Preventative Education, Community Development, Counselling and Home-Based Care, and at the same time invite Zambian ladies to help us in these apostolates. In deep trust we hope to accept the first postulants in 1993 as we have some aspirants working with us this year. [4]

Referring to the increased expenditure involved in the new direction the Zambian ministries would take, Sister John Vincent added:

> With regard to finances, all our missions are completely supported from the Mother House.[5]

In writing this, she acknowledged the Sisters on the home missions, who continued to work hard to maintain resources from their varied works of caring for the sick in hospitals, in homes for women and children with special needs and in schools at all levels.

Sr. Angelo Roncalli describes the turn of events:

> Around this time at the beginning of the last decade of the twentieth century, the central leadership of our Congregation decided to accept local candidates into the Congregation. This was a reversal of an earlier decision against the venture. The main reason for this new thinking was that the future indigenous Sisters would help to respond to the growing epidemic at a time when European Sisters were thinking of returning home after many years on the missions. There would be a new approach adopted in health care which would be home-based, and the Sisters would no longer staff the hospitals but work among the people in villages and compounds. With this in view a second foundation was made at Chingola in the Copperbelt.[6]

Sister Eileen McLoughlin, recently arrived from the U.K. to serve on the Vocations Recruitment team, distributed leaflets about the Congregation at the Parish Vocations Club. Sister Anne Griffin was the named contact Sister. Three girls from the club approached her to serve the Congregation on a voluntary basis. One of the girls was aged sixteen, the others were both aged seventeen.

Among the AIDS related ministries springing up in Zambia in 1991 was the service to orphans whose parents had died prematurely from the disease. In most cases, grandparents, aunts, uncles, or older siblings were their sole guardians. At the request of Bishop Telesphore Mpundu of Mbala Diocese, the Sisters at the Mbala Convent identified the major needs in their local area. Sister Mary Costello and Sister Anne Griffin, both nurses at the Government Hospital, undertook the task of finding out who and where the orphans were and what kind of needs they had. Sister Mary Costello describes how this project began:

> A glaring need at Mbala at this time was a survey of the Orphan situation and it was quickly decided in the community to start on this project as soon as things had been properly sorted out with the Church leaders.[7]

With the Bishop's and Parish Priest's approval, and working with the St. Vincent de Paul Society, the Sisters began their fact-finding task after receiving a list of seventeen names. On arriving at the compound

> they saw all the children and could get a rough idea of their nutritional status and obtain information whether or not the children were at school. If not, why not?[8]

Sister Mary Costello commented:

> We believe it is unethical to make a survey without responding to immediate and urgent needs. In some cases this was food. This at once brought us into another area – preparation of porridge and milk using soya beans. The three girls were very much involved in this. The local Church, St. Paul's, and the Convent offered land for the cultivation of the beans, and the Parish Church arranged for the Altar Boys Club and the Vocations Club to till this.[9]

Chapter 15 – Racing Towards the Finish

The problem of clothes was taken up by the St. Vincent de Paul Society who were generously helped from

> the wonderful containers that Sister Devota organised (everyone in Dagenham had to beware that the weekly washing didn't end up in Chilonga or Mbala) and sent to us by the Congregation. We sorted food and clothes parcels for the families, but unfortunately, due to extreme poverty, most of the orphans did not manage to get a share of what the family received; they remained severely malnourished and dressed in rags.[10]

Sr. Anne Griffin continues the narrative and relates how she and Sister Mary Costello directed this project into the future:

> As the numbers grew we realised that something more had to be done and after prayer and discernment in the community we decided that the best thing would be a day centre where the orphaned children could have at least one nutritious meal per day, could bathe and wash their clothes, do their homework for school and learn the basics for self-reliance, caring for younger dependent siblings, vegetable gardening, keeping chickens and other simple life-skills. We wanted a centre where everyone could feel at home, and where other children would not be jealous of the orphan children. At this stage, however, we had no funding – only ideas![11]

But help was near at hand. The well-known Irish Charity, Irish Aid, had representatives at that time working at Kasama, a township about a hundred miles away. The Charge d'Affaires, Brendan Rogers, was given accommodation at the Mbala Convent since there was no hotel in the town. He showed an interest in the orphans' project and asked about the Sisters' plans for the future. Sister Anne Griffin continues the story:

> When we explained the orphans' situation and how we wanted to respond to it, he mentioned that if we could manage to budget for twenty thousand pounds or less he could approve the project and we could get going without the bid having to go all the way to Dublin for approval. Talk about an answer to prayer! We quickly drew up a proposal for a building on our own grounds as we had more than enough space, separating it from the convent with a wall so there would be a level of independence for both groups.[12]

This fairytale story was further enhanced when four volunteers arrived from Ireland, one an engineer, another a carpenter. Both supervised the building. Two nurses helped to organise the centre based on health and safety guidelines. All the facilities were under one roof: a kitchen with simple wood-burning stoves, a food store, an office with a spacious store for non-food items. A large open-roof area provided space for the children to eat and do their homework; a separate block for showers and toilets. A section of the grounds was marked off for chickens and ducks and a rabbit shed. (The rabbits never took off!)[13]

Sr. Anne continues her description of the birth of the project:

> The network of volunteers was further helped by men from the U.S. Airforce, who were training the Zambian Airforce personnel at the time. The U.S. Servicemen brought along prisoners from the local gaol who provided labour for the water system. These men enjoyed their break and wanted to do 'hard labour' at the convent![14]

The special centre for the orphans was given the name 'Sunsuntila', suggested by Bishop Mpundu (now Archbishop of

Chapter 15 – Racing Towards the Finish

Lusaka). The name in the local Bemba language means 'to comfort' or 'to cradle' the baby. Sr. Anne Griffin agreed:

> We all thought that this was appropriate, as that is exactly what we wanted to do – comfort the bereaved orphans and set up a centre that would be an example to others.[15]

The 'Sunsuntila' success story reflects the vision and sensitive planning of Sisters Mary Costello and Anne Griffin, who created a project that lasted long after their moving on to other missions. For over twenty years the centre has continued its special ministry to the most vulnerable children. Sister Anne summed up her gratitude:

> God provided all that we needed to respond to the need then, and sent many people to help us both local and from abroad. The money was generously given for the building without any great problem and supplies that we needed just seemed to arrive. It was a blessed time and I thank God that Sunsuntila is still going and still offering care to those most in need.[16]

Another Health Care Ministry which began in 1991 was Education for the Prevention of AIDS/HIV. Centres for this were situated in the Copperbelt towns of Ndola, Mbala and Chingola. When Sister Una Brigid Mulvey (a qualified nurse and midwife) arrived in Ndola in 1991, she joined Sister Edith Woods in the work of the Home-Based Care Clinics in the compounds. Sister Una also directed teachers' workshops for AIDS/HIV prevention. Supporting the Sisters in this ministry was Maureen Wilson, the first volunteer. Sister Louise Mulhern, a professional counsellor, joined the AIDS Counselling Team at Ndola Central Hospital where Sister Eileen Keane (a Holy Rosary Sister) was a consultant physician.

Counselling AIDS patients and their families is a specialised skill and great sensitivity is required to address the fear that often surrounds the disease.[17]

At Chingola, Sister Mary of the Sacred Heart, Sister Lynn Walker and Associate Sarah Craze set up a Home-Based Care Project that was to develop and expand well into the future. As a midwife with long experience in Zambia, Sister Mary of the Sacred Heart was competent helping mothers with their pre-natal and post-natal problems.[18] Sarah Craze put her Drama talent to good use, helping through Drama and Drama Therapy, Marriage Guidance and Counselling. Sister Lynn soon became Director of the Copperbelt Health Education Project (C.H.E.P.) This non-Government Organisation provided workshops for AIDS Education for women and help for unemployed young people. By the end of 1992, Sister Lynn had already directed eighty workshops for factory workers on the shop floor.[19]

At the Midwifery School in Chilonga Hospital, Sister Rosalie Dunne established an AIDS Team in which she was directly involved. Her clients included parents, young people, Parish Council Members, secondary school pupils and rural health care staff. Sister Rosalie was to play a crucial role in the advancement of the health care system in the years ahead.

Sister Una Brigid's other ministry was to carry out the 1990 Chapter mandate to invite Zambian candidates to the Congregation. Recruitment began in four stages:

1. Involvement of Aspirants in the various works of the Congregation.
2. Sharing the Charism of the Congregation through presentations, talks and/or prayer in schools, Churches and Vocation Clubs.

3. Initiation into our prayer and community living.

4. Provision of time set apart for discernment and reflection.[20]

By September 1992, there were ten young Zambians interested in the Congregation's expression of Religious Life. Accommodation was prepared for them at Mbala Convent, where several rooms were added to the existing building. A formation programme was drawn up and Sisters in the Formation Team were sent on preparation courses, such as the Bemba Language School at Ilondola, where they could also learn about the customs and traditions of the Zambian people. The anthropologist and historian, Father Hugh Hinfelaar, a Missionary of Africa (White Father), presented regular seminars on inculturation or "the rooting of Christ's Church in Zambian soil."[21] As the Sisters of the Sacred Hearts prepared to receive young women into their Congregation, they were very aware that they were entering uncharted waters.

Alongside the recruitment of Religious Vocations was the effort to attract associate members and volunteers who would assist the Sisters in their varied and fast-moving projects. Finding suitable men and women who would work within communities was not easy. In some cases, the age gap and culture were too great. Some associates could be critical of the Sisters' way of life and vice versa. We can gauge the tensions from the Minutes of a Community Meeting:

> We must adapt to and accept the challenges the Associates present. It would appear that the question of volunteers has been rushed through without sufficient consultation… What is the purpose of sending these young people to Zambia without training or experience? They are an extra burden. The whole question needs reappraisal…

> The convent is like a tourist agency with all the comings and goings of these young people.[22]

These, however, were teething problems and, as the need arose, many Associates/Volunteers were engaged in an amazing variety of activities.

As Sister John Vincent had predicted in 1990 – "we will be talking about expanding." Two new foundations were made in the capital, Lusaka, one at Lake Road, the other at Kabwata. Lake Road, conveniently situated near the Airport, facilitated the frequent movement of Sisters to and from the U.K. and other destinations. Shortly after establishing this Convent, Sister Patricia McNulty, Regional Superior, died (17 July, 1994) en route to an Inter-Chapter Meeting at Chigwell. Her sudden death was a shock to the Sisters as she had been closely involved in all the regional projects that were that were springing up in Zambia at that time.

The longest established house in Zambia, Chilonga, was designated the house for formation. Here, on 1 May, 1994, Sister Mary Ita Emperor received the first Zambian postulants into the Congregation. Their names were Annie Chicanji and Cecilia Mulenga. Their first Profession took place on 1 February, 1997 at the Chilonga Mission Church, newly built with the help of a large donation of £20,000 from the Chigwell Mother House to the Treasurer of the White Fathers. This historic event involved the local parish community and the Sisters of the Region. The people raised their voices in song, danced and beat their drums in thanksgiving to God for the two young women who dedicated their lives to His Service. The formation team, Sisters Mary Ita and Marie Louise, witnessed their first candidates take this important step towards commitment to the Religious Life.[24]

Chapter 15 – Racing Towards the Finish

As part of the gradual handing-over of posts of responsibility at Chilonga Hospital, Sr. Kathleen left her work as Sister-in-Charge of the Maternity Unit, where she had spent nine years. Referring to some memorable events before returning to her native California, she wrote:

> The years passed and many of the highlights I remember with ease. The largest number of patients I ever had under my care at one time was in 1989 when I had sixty-four patients, twenty-three babies, forty-one mothers. This large number included mothers awaiting delivery. So with ten prenatals, several sets of twins in the ward along with their mothers, and then all the premature babies in the nursery and their mothers. Well, there were a lot of patients![25]

Over the years, the Sisters had witnessed a growing confidence among Zambian mothers choosing to give birth at the hospital, as Sister Kathleen's statistics indicate:

> When I came to Zambia in 1983, the average annual birthrate for Ward 6 was less than four hundred babies. By 1992 this had increased to over nine hundred. This was because the women trusted the hospital more and more.[26]

The General Chapter held in July, 1996, had as its theme: "Forward in Hope: Re-founding through Collaborative Ministries." Sister John Vincent was re-elected at this Chapter. In her Report, she referred to the "Revitalisation" theme of the 1990 Chapter, pointing out what had been achieved in the Congregation and that "far from coming to an end, Revitalisation needs to be intensified and expanded."[27] The Charism of the Congregation, she said, needed to be "restated in contemporary terms", interpreted as "Jesus Christ and the poor", expressed in "practical compassion and action for Justice and

Peace". If Re-founding was to become a reality, we had to follow the leadings of the Holy Spirit and continually to read afresh the signs of the times in order to discover deeper and greater insights with regard to our Charism. We need to focus on the future rather than concentrate on the past, like St Paul, who says: "I forget the past and race towards the finish".[28]

Addressing the Zambian Mission, and in particular the Vocation Ministry, Sister John Vincent pointed out:

> Our state of transition made it necessary to grasp the passing moment. In Zambia, the incidence of AIDS/HIV was a clear case to do with what no one else in Zambia was doing at the time, combined with the knowledge that we needed Zambian Sisters to work alongside us.[29]

The final years of the twentieth century saw a sudden rise in the number of Zambian vocations to the Congregation. There were three novices in Chilonga with Sister Mary Ita and ten postulants in Mbala with Sister Anne Kieran. Sister Una Mulvey's recruitment efforts were bearing fruit – her visits to parishes, secondary schools and 'Come and See' programmes. At this stage, it was necessary for the Congregation in general to have a clear understanding of the meaning of 'inculturation' in the context of its new members, in order to appreciate cultural differences.

It must be remembered that this period of intense activity and development took place against a background of great political upheaval in Zambia. From 1991 to 2002 the country was governed by President Frederick Chiluba of the Social Democratic Movement for Multi-Party Democracy. He replaced Zambia's first President, Doctor Kenneth Kaunda (1964), of the United National Independence Party. Zambia was a young nation and understandably its journey to democracy was not always a smooth one. The change-over of political parties created disturbances and often violent encounters. Sister Una, who travelled widely throughout the country, recalls:

> Travelling was dangerous and bandits were a threat, especially on the Great North Road, notably around the Serenje area.[30]

However, the Sisters of the Sacred Hearts remained undeterred. As the various projects expanded, new personnel, including Sisters and lay Volunteer/Associates happily increased. The Health Care ministry made rapid strides in Education for AIDS prevention and in Home-Based Care. Sister Maureen Gavin, who came from the U.K. to the Copperbelt town of Ndola in 1996, wrote of her first experience:

> In July I went to Ndola to learn from Sister Elizabeth Mooney about Home-Based Care. We worked in Chipulukuso, Nakwasa and Ndeka. These areas were chosen because the people were destitute. They received medicine, food and help with school fees from us. Once an area is chosen then the people there are asked to form groups of volunteers, 'fetentes', so they can help us find those who need help, and also assist with translating if the people don't know English. We visited some of their homes while others came to a central point or clinic where we could see more people in the allotted time.

> At Chingola, also in the Copperbelt, our community bought a house in Freedom Way, where a volunteer, Ian Kilcrest, lived. He walked the streets of Chingola to gather the vulnerable street children and to find out their needs. They told him: "Food, Shelter and Education". With the help of a group of unemployed Zambian people who

knew some English, Ian set about starting a school in an open space under a tree. Soon a local political building was put at his disposal. When Ian returned to Scotland, a new volunteer, Frank McGuire, took on the running of the school, which later became known as 'Kachema Musuma', meaning 'Good Shepherd'.[31]

As previously mentioned, Sister Rosalie Dunne, Midwifery Tutor at Chilonga Hospital, had organised an AIDS Prevention Project there. In February, 1997, she moved north to Mbala to set up a similar but larger one. At that time, Sister Angelo Roncalli was Superior at the Mbala Convent, overseeing many projects operating "from two tiny offices in the grounds". She continues the narrative:

> Sister Rosalie Dunne. A Legend! She came to Mbala in 1997 to set up an outreach programme to try to cope with the fall-out from the AIDS/HIV pandemic. The needs were manifold: orphans, widows, AIDS testing and counselling, health education, malnutrition, children out of school, poverty because parents were dying and leaving whole families with no means of income. Grandparents were stretched to their limits, government aid was non-existent.
>
> Sister Rosalie was first and foremost an excellent midwife, so naturally her first instinct was to look after the mother and baby problems. Many young mothers were dying and leaving behind infants with no means of sustenance. If there was an aunt or a grandmother, they would try to breast-feed the baby; if not the baby died. The problem was getting bigger every day, so the extended family network became overwhelmed. Tinned milk was available but too expensive for most people, or the risk of infection from dirty bottles was too great. With an excellent staff and financial backing from Irish Aid, CAFOD, the Caring

Chapter 15 – Racing Towards the Finish

Church in Scotland, the Rotary Club in Scotland, her family in Glasgow, Sister Rosalie set out on a multi-pronged approach to the challenge.

Health Education came first. She became famous (or infamous!) for her crusade against the spread of HIV infection. She set up an office with outreach to all Ministries, schools, churches, mother-and-child clinics, hospitals, Religious and Clergy. The programme consisted of education about the disease, the mode of spread, infection prevention, counselling and testing.

Next she looked at the Family and Village set-up. With the cooperation of Chiefs and Head men, she identified the villages that needed help. After doing some research, she presented the findings to various funding agencies for support. Thus was born 'The Village Support Group'. Working with the Ministry of Agriculture and the local Chiefs, land was identified and given to a group of orphans and their families. This group was then provided with a pair of oxen, a plough, seed and fertilizer. They planted crops which they harvested in due course. They sold some of the crop, thereby gaining an income, keeping enough to feed themselves. Out of the income they were expected to pay school fees and get the orphans back into education. The villagers were monitored closely to see if they complied with the rules. This involved visits to as many as twenty far-flung places deep in the bush. There were, of course, hitches, some killed the oxen for food or burnt the ploughs for firewood, or sold both! The solution to killing the oxen was donkeys. There were none in Zambia. Undaunted, Sister Rosalie went to the Ministry of Agriculture. Could she import them from Tanzania over the border? Off she set with a vet from the Veterinary Department, and the donkeys soon arrived at the Agricultural

Training Centre, Mbala. A training programme was initiated for their care, use and accommodation. People were selected from the villages and they came to the Centre to learn the necessary skills. The donkeys were eventually distributed around the villages. Thanks to Sister Rosalie, donkeys and carts became a familiar sight on the roads, doing work previously done by human hands.

The milk situation for new-born babies was still critical. A solution seemed simple, goats' milk. But this was taboo in Zambia, the people did not drink goats' milk! Sister Rosalie decided she would import pure-bred goats from Tanzania and educate the people on the goodness of this milk. The goats were imported and taken to the Agricultural Training Centre. Workshops were organised for training and caring for them. Eventually, after education on the benefits of this milk, the people accepted them.[32]

In 1956, Mother Antonia had regarded Mbala (Abercorn) as a favoured place. "It was," she wrote, "where we first set foot in Northern Rhodesia [Zambia]." During the closing years of the twentieth century, it is remarkable that the township became the focal point of such an extraordinary outreach to raise the quality of life for so many people in the territory. The members of the Religious Community that supported Sister Rosalie in her phenomenal range of undertakings were: Sister Angelo, Sister Cyril Donnelly, who fed poor people at the door and who had great influence on those in formation. Sister Anne Kieran, a competent and experienced Novice Mistress, Sister Francis Baker and Sister Sheila Fortune (both Sisters of St. Joseph from Canada), who directed dedicated and efficient Home-Based Care Centres within a radius of fifty miles. Sister Una assisted with education in AIDS prevention, at the same time laying the foundation of a basic school, partially funded

Chapter 15 – Racing Towards the Finish

by the Sisters of St. Joseph, which continues today under Government direction.

In her Report to the Chapter, 1996, Sister John Vincent envisaged new collaborators assisting the Sisters in continuing their Founder's Charism. By the end of the century this had happened. Not only were there new members of the Congregation, but the services rendered by Volunteers/Associates from England, Ireland, Scotland and Canada have a special place in the history of the Sisters of the Sacred Hearts of Jesus and Mary in Zambia.

Among the dedicated volunteers was Lynn Marquie, a young French-Canadian lady who was manager of the Sunsuntila Orphans' Centre. She loved and cared for the orphans and contributed greatly to the building up of the Centre. She obtained funding from the Roncalli Trust in Canada. This kept the day centre running long after Lynn's departure. Mary Alex Beaton from Scotland organised the Home-Based Care team in the Mbala district in conjunction with the Health Department and the hospital. This project was run from the convent and included a 'door ministry". Angela Curry from England, a trained Agriculturalist, has already been mentioned in relation to the crop cultivation for the orphans' project. Francesca Pordage, also from England, was a P.E. teacher at Mbala Secondary School. She worked with young people in the parishes through drama and sport and accompanied Sister Una on her travels, assisting with vocation workshops and 'Come-and-See' programmes.

It has been the policy of the Sacred Hearts Sisters in Zambia to collaborate where possible with the local authorities in Education, Health Care, Agriculture, Social Welfare, and with local Churches, Chiefs and head men. It has also been advantageous to network with Non-Government Organisations, for example, the World Health organisation, CAFOD, World Vision and Irish Aid. When Irish Aid moved their Administration Offices to Kasama from the shores of Lake Chila, they donated the entire compound buildings to Mbala Convent. This was a huge gift which provided accommodation for staff employed in Sister Rosalie's multi-faceted project.

As the end of the twentieth century approached, St. Paul's words, "racing towards the finish",[33] echoed by Sister John Vincent in the 1996 Chapter, had relevance for the Zambian mission where there was still much to be done. With the great 2000 millennium approaching, there was a sense of hope and expectancy that Sisters would be inspired to take the necessary risks to respond wholeheartedly to the call of "Jesus Christ and the Poor".[34]

Chapter 15 – Racing Towards the Finish

NOTES

1. MacDonald, Sister John Vincent. *Report to the General Chapter,* Chigwell: 21 July, 1990.
2. Corbett, Sr. Angelo Roncalli. *Article on Chilonga Hospital,* Chilonga: 1991.
3-5. MacDonald, Sr. John Vincent, op. cit.
6. Corbett, Sr. Angelo Roncalli. op. cit.
7-10. Costello, Sr. Mary. *Account of the Orphans' Project,* Mbala: 1991
11-16. Griffin, Sr. Anne. *The Sunsuntila Project,* Zambia: 1990s.
17-21. Mulvey, Sr. Una Brigid. *Account of Care of Patients with AIDS/HIV disease.* Zambia: 1990s.
22. *Minutes of Regional Meeting,* Zambia: 24 April, 1992.
23. MacDonald, Sr. John Vincent. *Inter-Chapter Report,* Chigwell, 1992
24. *Account of First Profession,* Chilonga: 1 May, 1994.
25, 26. Laverty, Sr. Kathleen. *My Zambian Experience,* Chilonga: 1992.
27-29. MacDonald. Sr. John Vincent. *Chapter Address,* Chigwell: July 1996.
30. Mulvey, Sr. Una Brigid. *An Account of Political Unrest,* Zambia: 3 April, 1996.
31. Gavin, Sr. Maureen. *Zambian Experience in the 1990s,* Ndola: 1990s.
32. Corbett. Sr. Angelo Roncalli. *AIDS/HIV Related Projects,* Zambia: 1990s.
33. St. Paul, *Letter to the Philippians.* 3, 12-14.
34. MacDonald, Sr. John Vincent, quoting the Founder, Fr. Victor Braun.

CHAPTER 16

Into the Twenty-First Century

*When we are dreaming alone it is only a dream,
When we are dreaming with others
It is the beginning of reality.*
(Dom Helder Camara)

AT THE DAWN of the new millennium, Sr. John Vincent sent this message with the Congregation's Calendar for the year 2000:

> It is an occasion of great hope but also one of deep fear. We do not know the changes that will take place within the world and within the Church in the next thousand years. We hope it will be a truly blessed time for humanity, that people and nations will live in peace and understanding, and make poverty and preventable sickness a thing of the past. We hope it will be a world genuinely transformed by God's justice and peace. We also fear that there will be no change for the better, and indeed that things may even change for the worst. There is, however, one thing we know for certain, although we will not be around to see it at the end of the millennium, God will!

Chapter 16 – Into the Twenty-First Century

> We invite you to join our Sisters in taking a bold and joyful step forward this New Year so that together we can go forward in hope. We take the hand of Jesus who makes the promise: *I am with you always till the end of time.* We do so in the assurance that his love never grows tired or dim with the passage of time. In the words of Saint Augustine: His love is ever ancient, ever new.
>
> Jesus is with us when we feed the hungry, clothe the naked, care for the sick, comfort the prisoner, welcome the stranger. His love never comes to an end. May his unending love inspire us to become ever more conscious of the hopes and fears, the joys and tears of all the people in our world, especially the poor, the sick and the lonely.[1]

In this message, Sr. John Vincent is clearly reiterating the Gospel principles on which the Congregation's diverse Mission is based – Home-Based Health Care, Clinics for AIDS/HIV patients, Community Schools for the poor and for Children with Special Needs, Counselling for Mental Health patients and their families, Skills Training for young people leading to employment, Centres for Orphans, Mother-and-Baby Clinics, Income Generating Schemes, Child-to-Child Programmes, participating in liturgies within the local culture, discerning religious vocations, serving in places where many people do not wish to go.

As mentioned in an earlier chapter, discerning indigenous religious vocations and the formation of young religious were 'unchartered waters' for the Sisters of the Sacred Hearts in Zambia. Nevertheless, by the year 2000 the Vocations Programme had made steady progress. New postulants had arrived in Mbala and novices continued their training at Chilonga. In 1999, Sr. Angelo Roncalli (Corbett) became Vocations

Promoter for the Zambian region, a role that presented many challenges. As a member of a team of Vocation Promoters for the whole of Zambia, she was able to access schools, colleges and vocation clubs in the different dioceses. The team followed a set programme with a specific theme which was circulated to every parish and Youth Leader. Meetings were held once a year. This Ministry involved travelling hundreds of miles and finding accommodation wherever possible, sometimes in remote, very basic rural settings. As a result of this work, many aspirants/postulants entered the different religious orders in Zambia. Retreats and pilgrimages were also arranged and young people had opportunities to meet and share ideas on the different aspects of religious life.

The number of postulants, novices and newly Professed Sisters increased significantly in the region and by the turn of the century there were two Sisters ready for Final Profession. They were Sisters Annie Chikanji and Cecilia Mulenga and the ceremony took place at Chingola on 8 December, 2001. Bishop de Jong of Ndola and Bishop Mpundu of Mpika (later Archbishop of Lusaka) were present at the ceremony. This was a landmark event in the history of the Congregation and Sr. John Vincent, whose term of office would finish within a year, described it as "a very wonderful occasion".[2] A new Regional Superior was also appointed at this time. Sister Anne Kieran replaced Sister Mary Costello, who, with Sister Catherine Kennedy, moved to Mukono, Uganda to found a new mission there. It will be recalled that both Sisters had made a unique contribution to the Health Care and Education Ministries since first coming to Zambia in the 1960s.

Sr. John Vincent's vision to 'expand' in Zambia continued to be realised. On 8 December, 2000, a new mission was opened

Chapter 16 – Into the Twenty-First Century

in Kasama, Northern Province. Kasama town is situated at a focal point, the main route being from Lusaka and the Copperbelt towns in the south-west and roads going westward to the Democratic Republic of Congo, and eastwards to Tanzania. The town enjoyed rapid development in colonial times and had its own airport, government hospital and schools. The new mission here was intended to become part of the growing number of small Christian communities living in the midst of poor people in a compound. Sister Mary Costello had chosen the house in consultation with the Bishop of Kasama. Sister Edith Woods and Associates Maureen O'Dwyer and Maura Dorling were asked to form a community there. This community, which consisted of a diverse group of members, was experimental at this stage and proved quite challenging. Sister Edith describes the early beginnings:

> We stayed at the pastoral centre while our house was being prepared. The house itself was like any other house in the location but needed some renovations: the blue gloss painted walls were to become cream, a toilet and shower had to be fitted, ceiling boards fixed onto the roof, fencing surrounding the house – security was a priority. The workmen lived in the house during the renovations and were overseen by Father Justin Mulengo, Vicar for Religious, who borrowed money from us to complete the job. The Motherhouse at Chigwell also lent the price of the house to the Archbishop, who purchased the building from Mr. Frank Mulengo.
>
> A big problem in Kasama town was its water supply. There were also too many pit latrines for a bore hole to be sunk, and we did not want to be so very different from our neighbours. So we had to collect water from the local taps for our needs. In time, we would have an underwater and

overhead tank with a pump. The water was supplied by the local council and had to be boiled prior to drinking. We were also advised to add chlorine. Rain water in the rainy season was collected in containers of all shapes and sizes arranged around the house.

The three of us moved into the newly renovated house, No.96C in Location on 23 November, 2000. It was the feast of St. Clement and that was the name of the small Christian community in our section. We introduced ourselves to the Community Leaders and attended meetings regularly, although we did not understand all that was said.[3]

Besides being a small Christian community in itself, the members quickly integrated into the other communities in Kasama, participating in liturgies and prayer gatherings and finding out what the local needs were. Sister Edith Woods, a nurse and midwife, experienced in Home-Based Care, began systematic visiting of the chronically sick people in the Location and in the surrounding villages. She was assisted in this work by local people and with funding from CAFOD and Irish Aid. Maura visited the villages looking for children with special educational needs. Gradually, she set up small schools to provide basic lessons for them. Maureen O'Dwyer developed a project for children with disabilities, working closely with a physiotherapist from Kasama General Hospital. She also set up a project for out-of-school children, also for food security for communities and their orphaned children. She succeeded in putting the small village schools for Children with Special Needs under the Ministry of Education, thus enabling this work to continue when there was a change of personnel in a few years. As already pointed out, this community was intended to be experimental. It has, however, gone from strength

Chapter 16 – Into the Twenty-First Century

to strength. Today, its outreach continues with young Zambian Sisters of the Sacred Hearts of Jesus and Mary responsible for its diverse apostolate.

This small Kasama community reflects the variety of services being offered in the more settled missions at Chilonga, Ndola, Mbala and Chingola. It became a challenge for Sister John Vincent and Sister Anne Kieran, the Regional Superior, who had to maintain communications with such far-flung missions, when telephone and electronic communications were still in the early stages of development. Despite the variety of ministries, it may be said that there was unity in diversity. In order to create cohesion, Sister John Vincent clarified the multifaceted apostolate under the heading of Parish Development rather than the title of Households in Distress (H.I.D.) This had been the umbrella term chosen by the Region to bring together the different strands of the apostolate undertaken by all the Sisters in cooperation with Volunteers, Associates, other Congregations, Government Departments, non-Government Organisations, Child-to-Child programmes and generally people of goodwill. Sister John Vincent developed the theme further:

> All the work involves different professional skills, for example, Nursing, Community Care, Preventive Health Education, Counselling, Community Schools, Teacher-Training, providing resources for children with disabilities, income-generating projects, care of orphans, skills-training for school leavers, pastoral care of the dying. It is intended that all these ministries be regarded as a whole. No one area is more important than another. No one can do this work alone. Each person who offers to help us in our apostolate, however young, old, skilled, unskilled, for a short or long period, has a contribution to make in a situation that is desperate.

Because of the nature of the apostolate, I term it Parish. Everyone is involved in the local church, whether at small community, parish, diocesan or national level.[4]

At the Mbala mission, Sister Rosalie's extraordinary range of projects, all of which were AIDS/HIV related, progressed with amazing success as the new century moved on. Although in poor health, she supervised the work involved in the new initiative for the provision of donkeys and goats. She was assisted in this work by Sister Sheila Fortune, a Canadian Sister of St. Joseph, now ministering to the Inuit People in Labrador. From Sister Sheila's detailed diary of events, we learn that in the early years following the millennium, Sister Rosalie

> entered into a contract with the Ministry of Agriculture and Co-operatives to house the Donkey Programme at the Farmers' Training Centre. The Households in Distress hired three workers to care for the donkeys, to breed them and prepare them for transfer to villagers caring for orphans and vulnerable children.[5]

In 2008, Sister Sheila wrote:

> Of the fifty-two Village Orphan Support Groups HID is assisting, thirteen have been trained in donkey traction. These animals are used for transport, ploughing and in some areas for cultivating and weeding. It is a joy to see how the villagers, and especially the children, bond with these *favourite* animals.[6]

Workshops were arranged to train groups from the villages in the care and use of the donkeys. Teams were formed from these workshops which taught people how to continue the care and training of the animals. The ownership of the donkeys was passed on to a Village Orphan Support group. Each group was

Chapter 16 – Into the Twenty-First Century

monitored for one year by a member of Sister Rosalie's staff to ensure that the donkeys were looked after and utilised well.

In the same way, the Dairy Goat project made remarkable headway, with several orphan support groups participating in it. It will be recalled that the aim of this project was to provide milk for babies whose mothers had died from AIDS/HIV. Again, workshops were arranged with a practical emphasis, so people became skilled in caring, housing, feeding and general hygiene. The expertise of the local veterinary service was also utilised. Referring to this project, Sister Sheila wrote: "We are becoming experts!"[7]

Funding for the many employees required to support the 'animal projects' came mainly from Sister Rosalie's own fund-raising efforts, her family in Glasgow, from CAFOD, Irish Aid and from the Motherhouse in Chigwell. One unfortunate event occurred in April 2004 when an armed gang entered the convent in Mbala at night and got away with cash which amounted to staff wages for a month. This was a traumatic experience for the Sisters, but thankfully none of them came to any harm.

In Lusaka, in the south of the country, further development was taking place. Associates Mark and Lucy set up a project for vulnerable children at Misissi, while at Kapwata, Associate Ursula ran a successful women's needlework club, giving training for employment to several young people. The treadle sewing-machines used were gifts from the U.K., transported in one of the large containers which came regularly from Europe.

The large project at Bauleni in Lusaka, sometimes referred to as 'The Street Kids Project', experienced phenomenal growth and development in the early 2000s. Six months before her term of office ended, Sister John Vincent gave the following account of her visit to Bauleni on 13 December, 2001:

I saw great developments in the work there. Sister Elizabeth Dawson has made great strides in fulfilling her vision for children with disabilities and the other vulnerable children. Alongside the formal teaching classrooms are the flourishing gardens, poultry and pig units. As well as being income-generating these are training places for young adults. At the same time Sister Elizabeth and her devoted team, and in co-operation with the Department of Education continue a regular programme of in-service training for Community School teachers and Home Based educators, as well as commitment to the Training College curriculum. At the present time she is working with other agencies that deal with orphans and other vulnerable children. There are plans to build fish ponds at Bauleni to supplement the daily diet. Sister Elizabeth hopes to establish a regular 'outward bound' type of holiday camp near Lake Kariba for children from Bauleni and other parts of Lusaka. Mr. Murphy, who was until last year the International Co-ordinator for the Street Children's projects, has already begun to work on the shared projects. Hopefully it will be well under way by next year and will be of great benefit to many poor children and young adults.[8]

Rapid developments were also taking place in the Copperbelt town of Ndola. Seminars and training for adults were held in the well-equipped Chinika House. From here, Sister Elizabeth Mooney ran the Home-Based Care Service, of which she was project manager. She had also increased the income support for orphans, vulnerable children and widows. There was no irrigation system and in order to maintain a water supply during the eight-months dry season, she organised the digging of two wells on the orphans' and widows' farms. This made a great difference to the lives of the people, who could then grow vegetables throughout the year. From Chinika

Chapter 16 – Into the Twenty-First Century

House and also from the Iseni Welcome Centre in Chingola, the Sisters were busy distributing the contents of the World Food Programme to the surrounding villages.

Life on the missions can be full of surprises. On 18 January, 2002, a belated Christmas parcel arrived for Sister Elizabeth Mooney. Unable to collect it at the Post Office herself, Sister gave her postal slip and identity card to Sister La Salette. The Post Office refused to hand over the parcel and both Sisters were asked to report to the office of the Drug Enforcement Commission, where the Customs had opened the parcel which contained a Christmas cake. The Customs' Officers accused Sister Elizabeth of importing the drugs Mandrax and amphetamines in the cake. Both Sisters were refused legal aid and were put in the police cells at Ndola Central Police Station, and were detained there until the following day. It was thanks to the intervention of Bishop de Jong and the Vice-President of the country that they were released on police bond. They had to report to the Police Station three times between 16 and 18 January, when the police bond was cancelled. The results of the laboratory tests were not given.

Sister La Salette was eighty-four years old and had served in Zambia as a nurse and midwife since the first mission had been established in Chilonga in 1956. This experience, however, did not deter the Sisters from continuing the Health Care ministry at Ndola. They were staunchly supported by Bishop de Jong, numerous priests, religious and the faithful people of Ndola.[9]

The Congregation's first mission, Chilonga Hospital, was handed over to the indigenous Sisters of the Child Jesus in December, 2005. The convent had remained open as a house of formation until 2005, when a decision was taken to close it.

This was the mission where many Sisters had been introduced to missionary work in Africa and for them it held special memories. Sister Maureen Gavin, who ran the Home-Based Care ministry in nearby Mpika, and Sister Angelo Roncalli, with Mr. Mboa from Mbala, did most of the clearing of the house. After fifty years, this was no small task! Sister Angelo records the final moments:

> I closed the door for the last time and handed over the keys to Father Waldemer, the Polish parish priest, in December, 2005.[10]

Sister John Vincent's twelve-year term of office came to an end at the General Chapter in Chigwell, July, 2002. Her successor was Sister Catherine Collins. Before the Chapter, Sister John Vincent carried out an evaluation of the Zambian Region under a Five Core Ministry Plan: Health Care, Education, Pastoral, Development and Congregational. Although there was positive recognition of achievements over the years, some urgent questions were raised. One of the most critical was training provision for young people to prepare them for worthwhile employment. Another issue was the formation of new Zambian postulants and novices and whether this should take place in their own country or in an International Centre. The constant turnover of Sisters and Associates in communities was another concern. Many Sisters believed it would be good to have a core community to give stability and support. Different models of Community needed careful monitoring.[11]

The end of Sister John Vincent's administration in August, 2002 may be described as the end of an era. Her vision for Zambia was unique and her commitment equally outstanding. She left a legacy that will live on. Despite failing health, she returned to Ndola, where she hoped to resume work for mothers and children at Chinika House. On 12 October, 2004, she left Zambia for good. Sadly, on the evening of the same day she died, soon after her arrival at London Airport. She will be remembered for her total dedication to the people of Zambia.

NOTES

1. MacDonald, Sister John Vincent. *Message to the Congregation*, Chigwell: Calendar 2000.
2. ibid. *Circular Letter to the Sisters of the Congregation*, Chigwell: 2002.
3. Woods, Sr. Edith. *A New Foundation*, Kasama: 2000.
4. MacDonald, Sr. John Vincent. *On Ministries in Zambia*, Chigwell: 2001..
5-7. Fortune, Sr. Sheila (St. Joseph's Sisters, Canada). *Diary for the Donkey/Goat Project*, Labrador: 2008
8. MacDonald, Sr. John Vincent. *Circular Letter to the Sisters of the Congregation*, Chigwell: 13 Dec, 2001.
9. Ndola Convent, *Journal*, Ndola: 18 Jan., 2002.
10. Corbett, Sr. Angelo Roncalli. *Closure of Chilonga Convent*, Chilonga: 2005.
11. MacDonald, Sr. John Vincent. *Circular Letter to the Sisters of the Congregation*, Chigwell: 2002.

Chapter 17

A Bold and Joyful Step Forward

THIS HISTORY is an attempt to record the story of fifty years of dedicated service given by the Sisters of the Sacred Hearts of Jesus and Mary to the people of Zambia. More than half a century has elapsed since Mother Antonia made a historic visit to Chilonga in September, 1954, where, with Bishop Van den Biesen, she "selected the site for the hospital". During this time, astonishing changes have taken place in the Church, brought about by Vatican II, and in Society, as a result of scientific and technological developments. In common with all Religious Congregations, the Sisters continue to adapt to these changes, as they strive to interpret their Founder's charism in the context of the 21st century, and to plan for the future.

In 2004, the newly appointed Regional Leader in Zambia, Sister Elizabeth Dawson, made her first Visitation Report[1] after visiting all the convents there. This Report took the shape of a consultative document, and it reflected the problems and concerns preoccupying the group of about twenty-eight Sisters dispersed in six convents in the Region. One of Sister Elizabeth's main questions was based on the quality of community life. With ageing Sisters and fewer numbers, she considered the question of the Sisters being overstretched trying to meet the needs of the various apostolates. Was the involvement of Co-Workers, Associates and Volunteers sufficient to ease the burden? It will be recalled that such concerns were not referred to by Mother Antonia in 1954, when she wrote to all the Sisters in the Congregation asking for volunteers for the new 'African mission'. In the aftermath of World War II, there was a large influx of religious vocations in Europe, enabling Religious Congregations to spread to distant places where there was an urgent need for Education and Health Care Services.

As the Sisters moved into the second half-century of their Zambian mission, Sister Elizabeth noted several areas that required close attention. One of these was the Vocations and Formation Programme. She noted that

> more consultation is necessary before we accept postulants/associates as our recent experience both in community and in the apostolate has been difficult.[2]

Sister Elizabeth is referring to the practice of sending newly professed indigenous Sisters to the U.K. for apostolic experience and training. In some cases, this did not serve the purpose intended and some Zambian Sisters left the Congregation altogether. Selecting an appropriate place for religious formation in their own culture proved problematic since it had been decided to close the present location at Chilonga, which was considered too remote. Ndola was chosen instead. Here there was easy access to formation and academic courses and wider opportunities for apostolic experience.

At the beginning of the consultative document, Sister Elizabeth commented:

> Having an overview of the Region makes me realise what a wonderful mission we have here in Zambia, and just how many people are being ministered to by us as Sisters, Postulants, Novices, Associates and Co-Workers.[3]

The main thrust of this document was to enable the Sisters in the region to make informed decisions for the future. A recurring theme is 'Community':

> Should we be looking at new forms of community e.g. the L'Arch type and other models which we have not yet explored and which were suggested in the Congregation's Apostolic Plan at the General Chapter 2002?[4]

At the Regional Meeting held in Dar-es-Salaam, Tanzania, 13 to 16 February, 2003, it was agreed to experiment with the L'Arche model of community.[5] Kasama seemed to be the ideal place to initiate a pilot project. One of the reasons for this was that Sacred Heart Associate, Sarah Cleary, (Special Needs Ministry), was considered a suitable person to begin the project as she had a love for and experience with children who had special needs. The house would require some adaptation for children with severe disabilities. If this project materialised, Aspirants and Postulants would have experience of apostolic work in this community, as it would follow the guidelines of a L'Arche community in which a life of prayer would be an important dimension. The project would be monitored during the pilot stage by the Regional Leader, Sister Elizabeth Dawson, and the Regional Administrator, Maureen O'Dwyer, Sacred Heart Associate.

The Home-Based Care Ministry (HBC) continued to go from strength to strength. Sister Elizabeth Mooney, who started this work at Chilonga in the 1970s, also established it in Ndola,

Chapter 17 – A Bold and Joyful Step Forward

from which she directed several services in outlying stations. Sister Maureen Gavin served Chilonga and the surrounding areas at Mpika and Chalabesa. This mission was not destined to have a long-term future with the pending closure of the Chilonga convent in 2005. At Chingola in the Copperbelt, Sister Romana was due to retire but she agreed to stay on to administer drugs, a service appreciated by the HBC Administrator in the Ndola Diocese. After fifty years in Zambia, Sister Mary of the Sacred Heart handed over the care of the victims of Leprosy to the local Parish Care Group in Kasama. At Mbala, Mr. Nderereh, a Sacred Heart Associate, took over the direction of Sister Rosalie's multi-pronged apostolate related to AIDS/HIV issues, described in an earlier chapter.

Due to serious health problems, Sister Rosalie Dunn had to return to the U.K. in May, 2004. The Education Programme for AIDS/HIV prevention which she set up continued long after her departure. She left behind a legacy of medical research to enable exploration into the causes of the virus. She was tireless in her efforts to find ways of counteracting what has been called "the scourge of Sub-Saharan Africa". Her untimely death, 21 May, 2008, at Marian House Nursing Home, Uxbridge, London, left a great void in her family and in the Congregation's apostolate in Zambia. She will be remembered for her love and generosity towards the poor and the most abandoned of its people.

Sister Geraldine Lynch came to Zambia at the age of sixty-six, having taught for forty years in the East End of London. She had a passion for education and was determined to provide it for the children and young people in the Chilonga township. She set about building a village school by raising funds for the project among her friends and past pupils in London. Sadly, before the building was completed she had to return home. During her ten years in the country, she taught and trained several groups of postulants in preparation for their novitiate, and regarded what she called her "Zambian experience" as a blessed period in her life.

The care of children orphaned by the deaths of parents from the AIDS virus continues to be a priority ministry, especially at Sunsuntilla, Mbala. The project, now with its own Board of Trustees, is placed on a solid foundation, directed by Sister Mary Ita and her Zambian Co-Worker.

The Jubilee to mark the foundation of the Chilonga Mission was celebrated in February, 2006. Two of the pioneers, Sister Mary of the Sacred Heart and Sister La Salette, returned for the event. Sister Kieran Marie had died on 19 February, 2005. Among the joys that delighted both Sisters was meeting five new Zambian postulants in Mbala and attending the ceremony of the Final Profession of five young Zambian Sisters. Both Sisters expressed their gratitude as they looked to the future with hope.[6]

Sister Celine de Jesu O'Keefe, who had been Director of the Midwifery School at Chilonga for eighteen years, retiring in 1991, gave her impressions on revisiting Chilonga:

> I had the privilege of revisiting Zambia in 1996. The changes, developments and projects were wonderful to see. It was great to see the Zambian Sisters of the Child Jesus occupying the main posts at the hospital and being salaried civil servants. The hospital was well-maintained, changes were made to meet the needs of the day, e.g. a complete unit for AIDS/HIV cases, and a badly-needed physiotherapy department, with two full-time physio-

therapists employed. There were no long-term patients now. With the BCG vaccination in the children's clinic, TB was virtually eradicated. It was a great joy to see such an achievement in so short a time.[7]

As the Sisters of the Zambian Region move further into the 21st century, the faith that inspired Mother Antonia has not diminished. They continue to grapple with the problems of declining numbers, the changing pattern of Religious Life itself, their ministries to the poor and disadvantaged, in order to forge a new way to respond to God's call and to the needs of the Church and Society. Under the Congregation's Leader, Sister Elizabeth Dawson, elected July, 2008, they accept Sister John Vincent's invitation to "take a bold and joyful step forward" into the future.[8]

Sister Celine's summing up of her visit to Chilonga in 1996 would seem a fitting way to conclude this narrative of the mission of the Sisters of the Sacred Hearts of Jesus and Mary in Zambia from 1956 to 2006:

> Years of joy and laughter, hardships and stress, ignorance and learning, loss and gain, grieving with the bereaved, loneliness, isolation and failure, intermingled with the joy of achievement, discovery and adventure. Such is the role of the missionary, to set up, develop, train, teach, empower. We talk about responsibility, give responsibility, prepare for hand over, process completed, hand over and move on.[9]

NOTES

1-4. Dawson, Sister Elizabeth, *Regional Report,* 15 April 2004.
5. *Regional Meeting,* Dar-es Salaam: 13-16 Feb., 2003.
6. McCaw, Sister La Salette, *Letter from Zambia,* Feb., 2006.
   McManus, Sister Mary of the Sacred Heart, *Letter from Zambia,* Feb., 2006.
7. O'Keefe, Sister Celine de Jesu, *Revisiting Chilonga,* 2006.
8. MacDonald, Sister John Vincent, *Message on Calendar,* Jan. 2000.
9. O'Keefe, Sister Celine de Jesu, op. cit.

* * *